Fillets of sole meunière 13.00

Fillet of sea bass, sauce vierge 13.75

Fried fillet of plaice, tartare sauce 8.50

Grilled turbot, beurre blanc 13.50

•

for two

Poulet de Bresse rôti 25.00

Côte de boeuf grillée, sauce Béarnaise 24.00

Canette rôtie aux pommes 20.00

Carré d'agneau persillé 20.00

•

Roast quails 11.00

Tête de veau, sauce ravigôte 9.50

Steak au poivre:

fillet 12.00   rump 10.00

Entrecôte marchand de vin 11.00

Sauté de veau aux morilles 13.50

Onglet sauté aux échalottes 9.50

Poulet poché à la crème et crêpes Parmentier 10.00

Tripes Lyonnaise 8.50

Ris de veau, beurre noisette 10.50

Boiled bacon with split peas and carrots 8.00

Grilled rabbit, mustard sauce 10.50

Carottes Vichy 90 Haricots verts 1.50 Roast onions 70.

Cabbage 70 Spinach 1.00

Pommes frites 1.25 Boiled potatoes 90 Mashed potatoes 1.10

Green salad 1.50 Chicory salad 1.25

Dinner menu, 1987

THE
BIBENDUM
COOKBOOK

OYSTER BAR

mpkin and 5.75 pancetta Soup	Bibendum Terence Conran Simon Hopkinson Matthew Harris	Roast rump of Lamb with couscous, babaganouch minted yoghurt 13.50 Takaki of tuna with niçoise and 13.50 Parmesane Mayonnaise

...ackerel with
...eeled cucumber,
...l and Mustard
...ressing 11.50

TERENCE
CONRAN
SIMON
HOPKINSON
MATTHEW
HARRIS

THE
BIBENDUM
COOKBOOK

PHOTOGRAPHY BY LISA LINDER
PROJECT CO-ORDINATOR TERENCE CONRAN

conran OCTOPUS

For Bill Baker, with love
1954–2008

First published in 2008 by Conran Octopus Limited,
a part of Octopus Publishing Group,
2–4 Heron Quays, London E14 4JP
www.octopusbooks.co.uk

A Hachette Livre UK Company
www.hachettelivre.co.uk

Distributed in the United States and Canada
by Sterling Publishing Co. Inc.,
387 Park Avenue South, New York, NY 10016-8810

Text copyright © Terence Conran, Simon Hopkinson and
Matthew Harris 2008
Classic recipes copyright © Simon Hopkinson 1994 as
featured in *Roast Chicken and Other Stories*, published by
Ebury Press, reprinted with permission
Design and layout copyright © Conran Octopus Ltd 2008
Illustrations copyright © Michelin Lifestyle Ltd, reprinted
with permission
Photography copyright © Lisa Linder 2008

Publisher: Lorraine Dickey
Managing Editor: Sybella Marlow
Art Direction and Design: Jonathan Christie
Photography: Lisa Linder
Production Manager: Katherine Hockley

ISBN: 978 1 84091 505 1

Printed in China

Page 1: Redundant ashtrays have now been recycled as butter dishes.
Page 2: Blackboards advertise the daily specials in the Oyster Bar.
Page 4 & 5: Energy at the pass in the Bibendum kitchen.

INTRODUCTION BY TERENCE CONRAN

Monsieur Bibendum rides again

I started my shop Habitat in May 1964 in a rather terrible building in Fulham Road, sandwiched between Draycott Avenue and Sloane Avenue and directly across from the wonderful Michelin building. Habitat remained there until the beginning of the Seventies, when shortage of space forced us to move to a converted cinema in the King's Road.

I had a sentimental attachment to our original ugly site so I converted it into the Conran Shop, where I could sell products that were rather more upmarket, singular and expensive than those sold in Habitat. I was also able to make the decisions myself, with just one buyer rather than going through the phalanx of opinions and decisions that I had to face as Habitat grew into a large international company.

However, the building that I really had my eye on was the Michelin building opposite. It appeared to be almost abandoned and was becoming more and more derelict as time went by. I dreamt about it as the ideal home for the Conran Shop of the future and wrote endless letters to Michelin's head office in Clermont Ferrand but to no avail. Then, one day in 1984, I heard that Michelin had put the building on the market. As there was quite a queue of people interested in it, I decided on the direct approach: I went to see the UK managing director and explained to him how

Previous pages: The staff of Bibendum with Matthew Harris, the head chef, in the foreground.
Opposite: The faience frontage of the Michelin building in Fulham Road.

important I believed it to be that the purchaser should restore the building with great care and sympathy. Because it was a listed building, the Michelin name would always be prominently featured on its ceramic façade and therefore would always be associated with Michelin. I promised that I would preserve and enhance the building and would top their best offer. He agreed and I bought the building.

About that time I heard that my friend Paul Hamlyn was looking for offices for his publishing company, Octopus, and so we decided to get together and share the development and ownership of the building. Octopus would have offices on the upper levels, there would be a giant new Conran Shop on the ground floor and in the basement – and perhaps most excitingly, a restaurant, oyster bar and café at the front of the building on the ground and first floors. A truly magnificent space and what I still believe, 21 years on and despite some spectacular new restaurant openings, is still the best space in London, if not the world.

It would have been madness not to have opened a restaurant in Michelin House, especially as the jovial images of Monsieur Bibendum, the symbol of Michelin, in all his bombastic energy and exuberance appeared all over the outside and inside of the building. The Michelin brothers had decided that encouraging people to travel in motorcars would hasten the development of motor travel and hence sell more tyres and what better reason to travel, especially in France, than to visit a restaurant. They launched a marketing campaign featuring Monsieur Bibendum that, in my opinion, has never been bettered. So Michelin kindly agreed I could use the Bibendum name after they had seen our designs and ideas for the space.

Now the serious business of planning the restaurant began and, of course, the very first decision was what type of food and therefore what sort of chef. I had a personal preference for the simple but delicious regional food that I used to enjoy as a young man in restaurants and cafés throughout France and particularly in the Lyon region, but which sadly today has almost disappeared. I didn't want to aim for Michelin stars as I have never found the rather pretentious food and surroundings necessary to achieve stardom to my taste. Equally, Michelin would find it rather difficult to award them to a restaurant called Bibendum in a building called Michelin.

As it so happens, I had met a young chef called Simon Hopkinson, who was working privately for the owner of a house I was trying to buy. We met socially on several occasions when he became the much-praised chef of a small restaurant called Hilaire, in Old Brompton Road. I discovered that his ideas about food coincided with mine but perhaps he preferred dishes to be a bit more complex as he had been a foot soldier for the Egon Ronay Restaurant Guides for several years. We discussed food and restaurants endlessly and realised that we shared many favourite dishes from around the world. I told him that I wanted to open another restaurant (I had opened the Soup Kitchens in the mid Fifties, followed by the Orrery in the

Graphics for the menus were taken from the mosaic of Monsieur Bibendum as he is featured in the ground floor lobby. Note how he is always smoking a Monte Cristo No 2 cigar – a sign of confidence, success and humour.

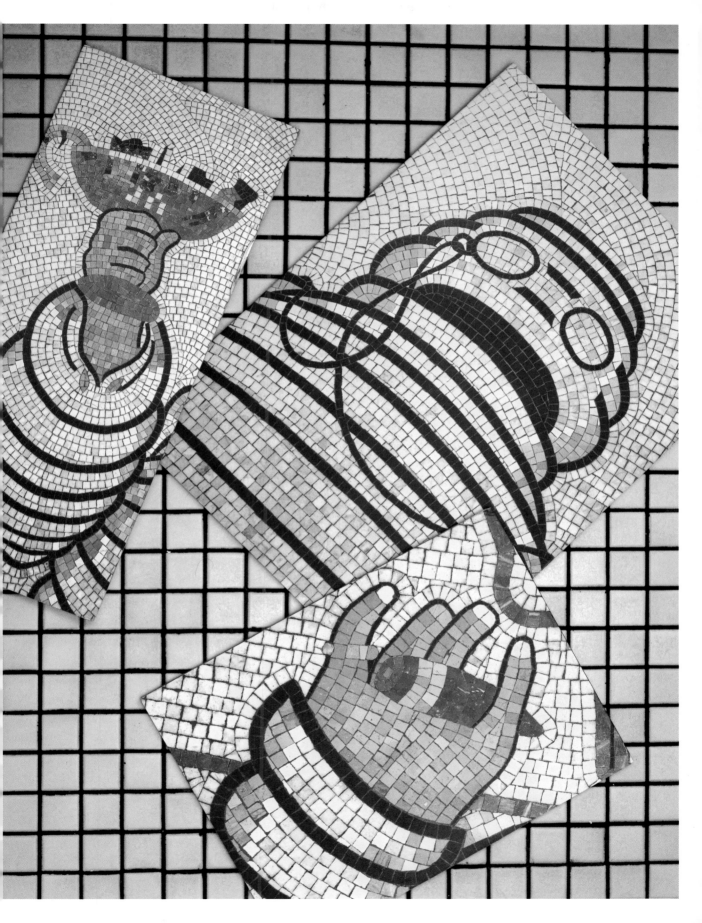

King's Road, and then in 1971 came the Neal Street Restaurant in Covent Garden, which was run by my brother-in-law, Antonio Carluccio. I had also designed restaurants for many other people.)

When I began negotiations with Michelin, I told Simon that this might be a once in a lifetime chance for us to build the restaurant of our dreams and to begin a restaurant revolution. I dined at Hilaire on the day I signed the contract and left a little drawing of a jubilant Monsieur Bibendum on the back of my bill with a note saying 'we have got it'. It's not a good idea to interrupt Simon when he's cooking unless you want to get roundly abused; that night I didn't!

Then the serious planning of the Restaurant, kitchen, Oyster Bar and Café began. This was quite a complex job as the building was in a very derelict state and had to be seriously modernised to accommodate all the different activities. Air-conditioning and extraction plus good drainage are essential and none of these previously existed. New plant rooms had to be installed, which necessitated two new floors being built on the roof of the existing building; the roof also had to be specially strengthened to take them.

Once we had established the basic plan for converting the building, such as where the entrance would be, how the goods would be delivered and rubbish collected, where the lavatories would be and how the kitchen would operate, it was all made much more difficult by the building being Grade 11 listed. This meant that existing staircases, tile and mosaic work had to be retained and restored. One change we were able to make was the installation of a lift from the ground floor to the first floor restaurant especially as both Simon and I hoped that our heroine, Elizabeth David, might become a customer. She lived nearby but was severely disabled and we felt she wouldn't be able to manage our stairs no matter how hungry she was.

Then there was the question of the kitchen. I favoured an open kitchen as I have always believed that the sight of chefs preparing food is reassuring and attractive to the customers. It also means that the kitchen staff keep the place clean and tidy and that the front of house staff don't argue with the kitchen, or vice versa. Perhaps my main reason was that I had worked in the appalling squalor of a French kitchen in a cellar and felt how depressing it was for the chefs never to see the customers enjoying what they had prepared. Simon disagreed. He preferred the comparative privacy of an enclosed kitchen to be able to robustly encourage his staff. He also thought that an open area might lead our customers to think they could interrupt the intense process of preparing and cooking food. He won. Simon took charge of planning and selecting equipment for cooking, dishwashing and storage, and I designed the Restaurant, Oyster Bar and Café, together with all the furniture that was made especially for us by Benchmark, and is still there to this day.

The waiters' station in the centre of the Restaurant and above it, the iconic stained glass window, which shows an ebullient Monsieur Bibendum raising a glass of nails, flints and broken glass.

So what about the style of the restaurant? We felt strongly that it should reflect the food, wine and service we offered. We decided that this should be a new animal, somewhere between the relaxed informal atmosphere of a Parisian brasserie and the precise elegant formality of a restaurant like The Connaught as it was at that time, as this would reflect the type of food that Simon and I had decided to provide. So, cloths on the tables and carpet on some of the floor, with a band of ceramic mosaic running through the centre of the restaurant under the huge waiters' station, on the front of the bar and right up to the two kitchen doors. This would also protect the carpet from too much wear and tear.

The charm of a restaurant comes from a myriad tiny details in its design. Here, of course, I had a huge amount of inspiration from the building itself with its newly restored stained glass windows, and the amazing creative brilliance that Michelin had put into the creation and development of Monsieur Bibendum over the years. It would have been difficult to go wrong. However, the ergonomics of restaurant design are fundamental to the comfort of the customers and to the efficiency of the waiters and commis. Serving food and wine elegantly in a small space requires skill, and clearing plates and dishes is just as difficult. If the waiters' stations are not thoughtfully designed with surfaces of the right dimension and height, it makes it difficult for the front of house staff to do their jobs well. Equally, if customers' chairs or tables are not the right height or dimension they will not be relaxed or comfortable.

Apart from using the ebullient curves of Bibendum subtly in the furniture, the glasses and decanters, and even having his image woven into the napkins and tablecloths, we used his graphic form on menus, wine lists and bills. We also produced postcards with images of the building when it opened in 1910 and a book about the history and reconstruction of Michelin House.

Two great bits of luck happened just before the opening. One was a portfolio of pictures of the great names in French motoring, circa 1900, done by an artist called 'Mich', rather in the manner of Sem. All the great names such as De Dion-Bouton, Delahaye, Louis Vuitton and, of course, the Michelin brothers were featured. They hang around the walls of the restaurant. Then I had a phone call from America and a voice said 'I very much admire what you are doing with the restoration of the wonderful Michelin building. I have been in the tyre business in America but I'm retyring (!) and I have these framed Michelin posters that I'd like to give you for your building.' A week later a couple of crates arrived with ten of the original early 20th century posters, beautifully framed. They immediately took pride of place in the Restaurant and Oyster Bar. Thank you, oh! thank you at least twenty times for your generosity.

The entrance of the building in Fulham Road had originally been the tyre bay where cars arrived and were weighed to decide which type of Michelin tyre should be fitted. Immediately beyond this was the touring office — where Michelin helped you plan your journey and sold you their wonderful guides and maps — and the

Many details were specially designed to reflect the Bibendum image. Clockwise from top left: waiters' station; mosaic bar front; café chairs with a Bibendum back; carafes; detail on the reception desk; silver wine bucket; loose chair covers.

salesroom with a magnificent mosaic floor with a giant Monsieur Bibendum puffing a huge Monte Cristo No 2 cigar. Around the walls are fantastic ceramic plaques depicting the late 19th century and early 20th century bicycle and motor rallies and races that Michelin sponsored or organised. Every motoring enthusiast is fascinated by them and they do depict a magical moment in the history of motoring. This area has become our Oyster Bar and Café serving drinks, simple cold food and hot soup, as well as oysters, crustacea and towers of plateau des fruits de mer. We also sell fish, lobsters and oysters (and fresh flowers) from a tyre bay. We have recently installed a simple espresso bar with croissants, patisserie, and delicious little bridge rolls with savoury fillings individually wrapped in greaseproof paper. Hot roast beef sandwiches have been another recent addition. The Oyster Bar and Café is the place

to come if you want a quickish lunch or supper, or just a cup of coffee for breakfast or a glass of Champagne and a patisserie with a friend whilst you are shopping in Brompton Cross, as this area is now called.

One of our ideas was to subtly change the atmosphere of the restaurant every season, so we change the loose covers on the chairs to different colours to reflect the time of year: fresh and cool for spring, warm for summer, rich for autumn, and classic and elegant for winter. This, together with the European walnut screens and waiters' stations with silver edges, marble tops, and marquetry inlays has given the restaurant a classic feeling that has not been materially altered since day one. I could go on writing endlessly about the thought, detail and discussion that went into making Bibendum happen just 21 years ago and of the many people who worked so hard as designers, architects and contractors that made it all possible.

We opened in 1987, a little later than planned – but who doesn't – and handed over to the original Bibendum restaurant team headed by Simon Hopkinson with both Henry and Matthew Harris (the current head chef) in the kitchen.

One of the remarkable things about Bibendum is the number of well-known and successful chefs who have been through the Bibendum learning curve and have gone on to achieve great things in their own kitchens. They include Jeremy Lee of Blueprint, Bruce Poole of Chez Bruce and Philip Howard of The Square. Joel Kissin, who came with Simon from Hilaire, was the original manager. He left to manage several other of my restaurants and Graham Williams took over, and together with Pierre Woodford has established a front of house style that has, through the years, charmed our customers with discreet elegance, efficiency and gentle humour.

Wine has always been important to Bibendum, and we have one of the very best wine lists in London, selected originally by Bill Baker then by Matthew Jukes, much admired by our customers and recognised by various awards. (There's more about our wines from Matthew on page 102.)

Bibendum may have added a couple of tyres to his waist over the years, but he and our restaurant remain as virile, energetic, and beautiful as we were the day we opened 21 years ago. A bit of experience hasn't done us any harm either. We have had people who have so much enjoyed their lunch that they have stayed on for dinner and of people who want to stay after dinner until breakfast the next day, but I am glad to say that for the staff's sake, these are relatively unusual.

A restaurant is rather like a theatre, no two performances are exactly the same

and you are usually performing to different audiences. Every day and every night the restaurant changes and will continue to do so, but I hope nobody will notice. Over the years the restaurant has been continuously refurbished – new carpet, new seat covers, repainted, re-polished – as, obviously, over 21 years of hard use even the best materials get the patina of age. We like this patina and believe it adds to the quality of the restaurant so we only revitalise where necessary. So many restaurateurs believe they have to make major changes if their restaurants are to be fashionable and up-to-date. But if it has been thoughtfully designed and equipped in the first place and well looked after, as Bibendum has, such changes are unnecessary and often upset loyal customers.

However, our food and wine do not remain static. New foods become available, new, perhaps better, sources of supply found, while new vintages produce wonderful new wines. Inevitably there are some staff changes but we hope that we keep the best staff in both the front of house and the kitchen. We spend time and care training staff to do their jobs even better. Let me confirm that the staff receive all the gratuities on top of their salaries so they are reasonably well rewarded for doing such demanding jobs. I also think that the fact that Michael Hamlyn, his sister and I own Michelin House is an advantage over many restaurants who suffer from avaricious landlords. This gives Bibendum a sense of security and makes it part of a community with the other tenants of the wonderful building.

We all want Bibendum to continue to succeed and we will do everything we can to make it the best and most pleasant restaurant in London – after all we now have the benefit of age and experience on our side.

Nunc est Bibendum et bon appetit.

Opposite: the barman in the Oyster Bar. Above: a simple meal of Poole prawns and oysters is typical of the fine seafood on offer in the Oyster Bar.

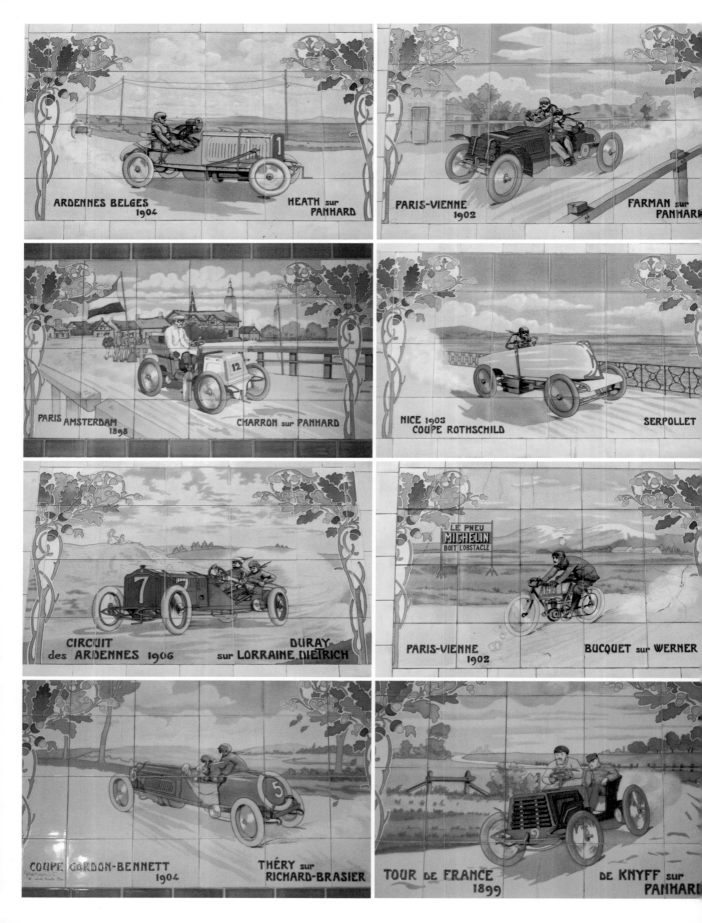

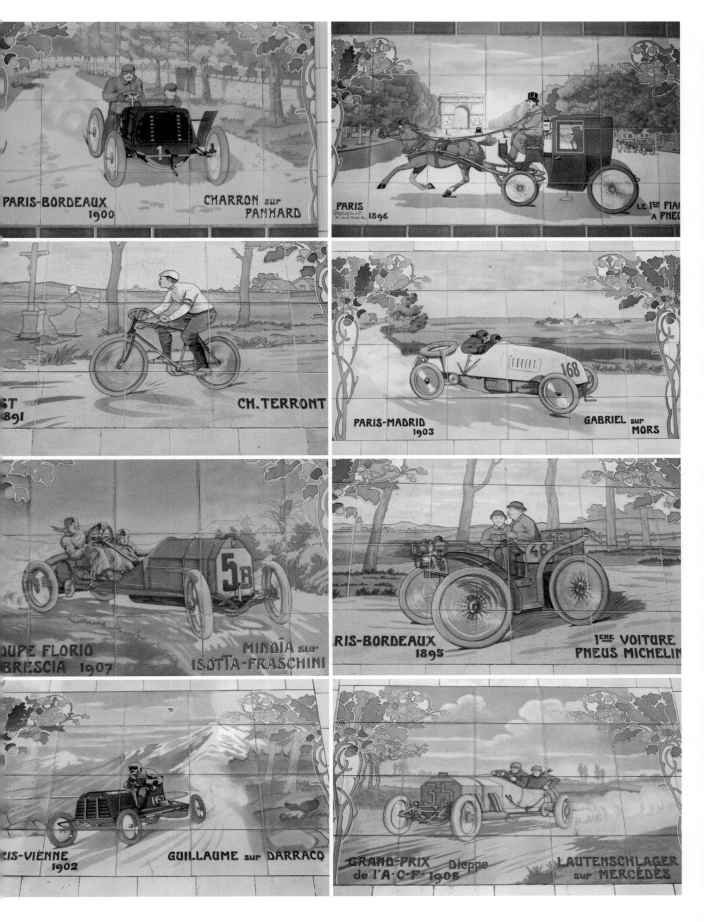

BY STEPHEN BAYLEY

The special marriage of tourism and food

Michelin had an opportunity and a problem. And the response to the former was the same as the solution to the latter. The opportunity? A successful French company making the most technologically advanced tyres in the world. The problem? Tyres are boring. Tyres are a marketeer's nightmare because they have no emotional attributes. Nowhere anywhere on the planet has anyone ever thought to himself 'Wow! I've had a great week. I must go and buy a set of tyres!'

So, Michelin played to its strengths of Frenchness and inventiveness. These Clermont-Ferrand industrialists construed the whole of France as a vast table laid with regional dishes. And the distance between courses was not measured in minutes, but in miles, or rather, kilometres. Meals became destinations and a restaurant became the rationale of a road journey. Everybody enjoys eating and travelling. That's obvious, but Michelin was the first company to turn wanderlust and appetite into an infallible business proposition.

The device which covered this epic insight was Monsieur Bibendum, a cartoonish hominid composed of tyres. At first he was a graphic, a poster boy, but he soon evolved into something more subtle: a company spokesman, even a symbol of all France and its seductive *l'art de vivre* (art of living well). To Monsieur Bibendum tyres were not rubber disposables, but connections to pleasure. The invention and deployment of Bibendum was one of the most inspired branding exercises of all time (a brand being a winning mixture of expectations and associations). But it was not the work of consultants with flipcharts and focus groups, but of the Michelin

Previous pages: The ceramic plaques that surround the ground floor lobby of the Oyster Bar depict rallies organized by Michelin to promote motoring. Opposite: One of the stained glass windows in the first floor restaurant.

brothers themselves. They did not do any research. They just acted with honesty, vision, commitment and consistency.

They loved France, food and driving so began to think of ways to connect them all in the customer's imagination. The first Michelin *Guide Rouge*, a gazetteer of French towns with tips about hotels and garages, was published in 1900 and distributed free. They only started to charge for it in 1920, but by that time Michelin's corporate genius for publicity – in the person of Monsieur Bibendum – had given it unquestioned leadership in the culture of road travel. They could charge what they wanted for this now indispensable guide to educated motoring, a little book that – uniquely and influentially – fused tourism and gastronomy.

At the beginning of the twentieth century Michelin helped define the potential

of the private car. Benz and Ford worked on the engineering, but Michelin understood how farting, wheezing and banging contraptions could become the ultimate consumer product. These were early days. Chauffeurs were so named because it was the driver's job to heat-up frozen carburettors on recalcitrant cars whereupon chilly passengers sat miserable under rugs, exposed to the climate. That first *Guide Rouge* carried ads for Peugeot bicycles as well as Peugeot cars: the future hegemony of the automobile was not obvious in 1900, least of all to those stranded passengers wondering where the next hot bath and good meal were coming from.

And, as ever with Michelin, practical considerations were dominant. The Michelin brothers' business was founded on their concern for the reliability of their tyres and the 1900 *Guide Rouge* has whole page instructive cross sections of a valve, printed with a surreal accuracy that predicts the erotic graphics of Francis Picabia and Max Ernst. The chauffeurs are given *conseils sur le gonflage* (advice on inflating tyres). But even in 1900 when your Renault or Panhard could not necessarily be relied upon to complete even the shortest journey, there is advice for the gastronome and hedonist. Once finished with inflating their tyres, the Michelin customer might inflate himself. The Hotel de France at Montreuil-sur-Mer in the Boulonnais is, for example, recommended with stars. Monsieur Nivert, whose business was to repair your bicycle, is given precisely the same accolade.

The 2007 Michelin *Guide Rouge* makes a fine contrast: more than 2,000 pages; city maps in colour; restaurant addresses are websites; and Lexus ads. It is, like all the best books, a delicious combination of fantasy and fact. Michelin *Guide Rouge* France gets you travelling on delicious journeys before you even move. The symbology has become brilliantly wrought – a star, a gable end, a parasol, a rocking-chair – which with spellbinding economy encapsulate any hotel or restaurant. Why not an arm and a leg to indicate extremely expensive establishments? Since 2000 the *Guide Rouge* has published critical commentaries as well. To describe a clientele as 'tendance showbiz' is witheringly brilliant.

And then there are those town plans: just opening the *Guide Rouge* at random kick-starts a reverie. Maubeuge may be a dump, but looking at the map has you restlessly wondering what a stroll from the Etang Monier to the Place de Wattignies might reveal. A wonderful little boulangerie, a bar, a chance romantic encounter. To have packaged, branded and successfully sold so much of the (often spurious) allure of travel is Michelin's distinctive achievement.

Of course, unglamorous rubber plays its part in this history of desire. The Michelin family was related by marriage to Charles Macintosh, whose discovery that rubber was soluble in benzine led to waterproof raincoats. The Michelin brothers were at first interested in putting rubber in the service of wagons and bicyclists, missionaries in the cause of pneumatics. Charles Terront used Michelin's new-fangled air-filled tyres to win the Paris-Brest-Paris bicycle race in 1891: three days and three nights of raw-bottomed cycling that made him France's first national sporting hero. Promoted by *Le Petit Journal*, the event became a public institution. Michelin tyres began to claim their place in France's imagination.

Michelin began to evolve an identifiable personality in 1894. Road-racing in automobiles joined endurance trials on bicycles in a contest for the consumers' attention. It was in that year that the Comte Albert de Dion (who later founded the Automobile Club de France) organised the very first road-race for cars. This was the Paris Rouen, and André Michelin was one of the competitors. It was also in 1894 that a defining insight occurred: when visiting the Universal and Colonial Exhibition at Lyon, the Michelin brothers saw the anthropomorphic potential of a pile of tyres. With arms and legs added, one of them said, it would look like a man. From that proto-surreal flash of inspiration was born Monsieur Bibendum, pneumatic man, herald of pleasure and progress. And of lunch.

Now began an astonishing story of brand-building, of corporate identity, although the Michelins never used such desiccated business school expressions. Instead, they intuitively understood the creative friction between image, desire, demand… and profit. In 1898 the illustrator Marius Rossillion (also known as O'Galop) turned the Michelin graphic insight into the famous pneumatic man. His name was taken from Horace's 'Nunc est Bibendum'.

Britain was an important export market. The expiry of rival Dunlop's patents gave Michelin the chance to realise their business priority of establishing a serious presence in the imperial capital. François Espinasses (1880–1925), an obscure member of the civil engineering department, was called upon to design Michelin House; apart from the Paris headquarters, no other building is known from him. Using Hennebique's

Opposite: Clear glass windows were specially etched with maps of French gastronomic towns taken from a 1910 Michelin Guide.

patent 1897 ferro-concrete construction (Robert McAlpine had acquired the licence for £300), the building was finished in a mere five months. But rapid erection was not Espinasse's greatest achievement. Michelin House was a bravura demonstration of untutored genius, a brilliant exercise in an indefinable style: part Nouveau, part Déco, entirely Michelin. Long before US developers had discovered the importance of corporate buildings being identifiable at 55mph from the freeway, Espinasses' idiosyncratic Style Bib brought kerbflash to London. Bibendum figures were meant to sit atop the corner turrets, but a timorous LCC objected. Still, in the best possible sense, Michelin House with its magnificent Bibendum stained glass windows performed as an advertisement.

So that means it is a building with a narrative. The famous encaustic tiles by Gilardoni Fils of Paris are based on drawings by Ernest Montaut. Thirty-four panels (comprising about twenty-four individual tiles each) show the very road-races that helped establish Michelin's reliability. These races were the laboratory where experiments on the development of the car and its tyres were carried out under intense press scrutiny. One panel shows the 1895 Paris-Bordeaux race where the Michelin brothers competed in L'Eclair, a car of their own construction with a Daimler chassis and a Peugeot engine.

A French amalgam of Art Deco, Michelin House opened 20th January, 1911. Fort Dunlop in Birmingham followed in 1916; the Firestone Building in the Great West Road, London in 1933. These are no longer used or have been demolished, but the splendid Michelin House was given a Grade II listing in 1969. In 1985 it was bought by Terence Conran and Paul Hamlyn and fully restored two years later.

The Great War interrupted Bibendum's expansion, but after 1918 the world was again ready to be peaceably explored. Travel was more arbitrary circa 1920: André Michelin had to argue for a rational system of road numbering. A 1921 English language Michelin brochure (with pretty cottage and rutted tracks) says 'Do you realise how much more enjoyable a well-prepared tour can be?' This was the developing genius of selling tyres by selling the desire to travel.

Bibendum leapt the species barrier in 1907 when journalist and epicure Maurice Edmond Sailland (1872–1956), known as Curnonsky, was sponsored by Michelin to write a weekly column in *Le Journal*, beginning 25th September. Called *Les Lundis des Michelin*, it was signed 'Bibendum'. This was the great inflatable's true debut as a public voice. From now on, Michelin was a company as adept at imagery as at technology. Its brand was as valuable as its production lines.

It is not quite clear to what extent Curnonsky directly contributed to the development of the *Guide Rouge*, although involvement is indisputable. But in a sense, he was the competition. Just as you find in whatever page you consult in Michelin *Guide Rouge* a note on regional specialities, so Curnonsky was himself drawing maps explaining in 1938, for example, that Thionville = *grenouilles au gratin*;

Belfort = *la queue de boeuf grillée* and Mulhouse = *carpe farcie*. Between 1921 and 1928 thirteen volumes of his *Guide des merveilles culinaires et des bonnes auberges françaises* were published. Then, in the 1930s Michelin enhanced its system by grading establishments with two and three stars and the expression 'Vaut le voyage' (worth a detour) soon after entered the language.

The 2008 Michelin *Guide Rouge* has gastromaps that take you right back to Curnonsky and his concept of the 'best culinary network in the world'. The twenty-first century reality of Nord-Picardie may be a hell of crowded autoroutes, Norbert Dentressangle trailers and Formula 1 hotels where even a Polish chambermaid would be a seductive exotic, but to Michelin readers it is a territory of dreams, a place where *moules*, *ficelles* and *flamiche aux poireaux* are commonplace.

But even if you are not going anywhere, Michelin's discovery and exploitation of that *sainte alliance* retains a voyeuristic pleasure for the stay-at-homes. Sit on your Eileen Gray Bibendum chair, a Michelin *Guide Rouge* in one hand… and say to yourself *maintenant il faut boire* (now, I need a drink). Thanks to Monsieur Bibendum, we are all gastro-nomads now.

The Oyster Bar lobby features a wonderful mosaic of Monsieur Bibendum in the floor – the inspiration for the restaurant's graphics – and ceramic plaques around the walls of motor rallies.

Classics

Recipes by Simon Hopkinson

Fierce heat in the kitchen keeps the chefs on their toes.

A truly wonderful taste of Italian sunshine. This recipe was introduced to me by a young chef who had worked at The Walnut Tree, in Abergavenny, Wales. He then spent a short time with me at Hilaire, in South Kensington (a small restaurant where I was chef previous to Bibendum) and suggested we might feature it on the menu. The original recipe comes from Elizabeth David's *Italian Food* and, frankly, is one of those dishes that spans all tastes: intensely savoury, lusciously oily and sweet and it also looks just terrific.

4 red peppers
4 garlic cloves, peeled
8 ripe tomatoes, skinned and deseeded
100ml/3½fl oz olive oil
16 canned anchovy fillets, drained
salt and pepper

SERVES 4

Piedmontese peppers

Split the peppers in half lengthwise and remove the cores and seeds. Season the insides lightly with salt and generously with pepper. Slice each garlic clove thinly and distribute between the 4 peppers. Place a tomato inside each pepper half, again season with pepper and a little salt. Place in a roasting tin, pour the olive oil over each pepper and roast in a preheated oven, 220°C (425°F) Gas Mark 7, for 30 minutes. Lower the oven temperature to 180°C (350°F) Gas Mark 4, and cook for about another 45 minutes or until the edges of the peppers are slightly burnt, and somewhat collapsed.

Remove the peppers from the oven and allow to cool before placing the anchovies in a criss-cross pattern on each pepper. Place on a plain white serving dish and spoon the juices over each pepper. It is essential to serve some good crusty bread for mopping-up purposes.

A busy lunchtime in the Oyster Bar. The chairs were specially designed to reflect Monsieur Bibendum's shape.

I cannot begin to wonder quite how many huge cock crabs we have boiled over the past 21 years, so producing the freshest and tastiest results imaginable. Live and kicking, here, means just that. This is a very sensible way to serve cold crab, separately enjoying the best of both the brown and white crab meat, with fragrant, soft green herbs contrasting nicely with the pungency of the coral-cream dressing.

white meat from a cooked 1.4–1.8kg/3–4lb crab
1 tablespoon chopped mixed herbs, to include dill,
    tarragon, parsley and chervil
juice of 1/2 lemon
a pinch of cayenne
4 tablespoons olive oil
salt

SAUCE
brown meat from a cooked 1.4–1.8kg/3–4lb crab
1 tablespoon tomato ketchup
1/2 tablespoon smooth Dijon mustard
1/2 tablespoon horseradish sauce
juice of 1/2 lemon
1 teaspoon anchovy essence
2 teaspoons Cognac
salt and pepper

SERVES 4

Crab vinaigrette with herbs

Mix the white crab meat with the herbs, lemon, cayenne and 2 tablespoons of the olive oil. Season to taste.

To make the sauce, in a blender, purée together all the ingredients and pass through a fine sieve. Depending on the 'wetness' of the brown meat, it may be necessary to thin the sauce with a little water. The ideal consistency should be like salad cream.

If you like neat plates of food, then divide the white crab meat into 4 portions and place in the middle of 4 plates, forming into circles with the help of a pastry cutter. Spoon the sauce in a swirl around the crab, and drizzle it with the remaining olive oil. If you prefer less structured food, then serve the white meat in a bowl and the sauce separately.

We prepare a lot of crab dishes every day for both the Restaurant and Oyster Bar. They arrive live as they must be freshly cooked.

Although I had first learnt to make the following intensely savoury beurre d'escargot at a French restaurant in Lancashire when I was 16 years old (during school holidays), it was not until many years later, on my first solo eating trip to Paris, that I first encountered the great big dish of snails served at the famous old bistro, Chez L'Ami Louis. It was their furiously hot and bubbling arrival at my table that instilled in me that, one day, I would also hope to offer up snails just like these in London. They have been on the menu, without exception, since day one.

48 canned snails
48 snail shells (these are usually sold together)
a large glass of white wine
a large pinch of herbes de Provence
salt and pepper

SNAIL BUTTER
450g/1lb unsalted butter, softened
50g/2oz peeled garlic, as fresh as possible, finely chopped
75g/3oz flat-leaf parsley, leaves only
25g/1oz dry breadcrumbs
50ml/2fl oz Pernod
1 1/2 tsp salt
1/2 tsp black pepper
1/4 tsp cayenne
5 drops of Tabasco sauce

SERVES 4

Escargots à la Bourguignonne

You will need 4 traditional snail dishes, each with 12 indentations, or, if wishing for smaller servings, dishes with only 6 indentations. Naturally, the butter recipe should then be halved.

To make the snail butter, put the butter and garlic in an electric mixer and beat together. Blanch half the parsley briefly in boiling water. Drain, refresh under cold running water, and squeeze dry. Chop this and the remaining parsley as finely as possible. Add to the butter with the remaining ingredients and beat together until thoroughly blended. Chill.

Place a baking sheet in the oven whilst it is heating to 230°C (450°F), Gas Mark 8.

Drain the snails and put in a pan with the wine, herbs and seasoning. Bring up to a simmer and cook for 10 minutes or so. Leave in the cooking liquor to cool, then drain. They are now ready to use.

One of Bibendum's most popular dishes – a cast iron dish of huge sizzling snails in garlic and parsley butter.

Firstly, using your thumb, push a small amount of snail butter (about half a teaspoon) into the bottom of a snail shell, then insert a snail, with its curved and pointed end uppermost. Gently push it further down into the shell and then top up with more butter – about 3–4 times the amount than before – and smooth off around the aperture of the shell, leaving behind a concave surface, so that, hopefully, most of the butter will remain inside the shell as it heats through in the oven. Repeat this process until all the shells have been filled. (If there is any butter left over, it freezes well.)

Place the shells on the dishes with their apertures as horizontal as possible. Arrange on the baking sheet and bake on the top shelf of the pre-heated oven for 15–20 minutes or until bubbling with gusto and smelling simply divine. Serve very much at once, with plenty of bread.

Work in the kitchen is intense and demanding. Above, snails sizzling on the stove.

The best onion tart is not simply about the onions… It is also very important that the quality and cooking of the pastry is carefully taken into account. However meltingly luscious and creamy the filling – and it must surely be just that – this would simply be a waste of time if it were not enclosed by a crisp and buttery tart case. If you can find them, I think white-skinned onions are the best ones to use here.

PASTRY
50g/2oz butter, cut into cubes
125g/4oz plain flour
1 egg yolk
a pinch of salt

FILLING
125g/4oz butter
4 large onions, thinly sliced
4 egg yolks
300ml/½ pint double cream
salt and pepper

SERVES 4

Onion tart

To make the pastry, quickly work the butter into the flour. Add the egg yolk, salt and enough water to form a firm dough. Chill for 30 minutes.

Roll out the pastry as thinly as possible and use to line a 20cm (8-inch) flan tin (make sure it's a deep one). Prick the bottom, and bake blind (see page 98) in the oven for 15–20 minutes or until straw coloured and cooked through.

Meanwhile, make the filling: melt the butter in a large saucepan, add the onions and a sprinkling of salt, and stew very gently, covered to begin with, without browning. When very wet and sloppy, remove the lid and carry on cooking on the same heat, stirring from time to time, until as much of the liquid as possible has evaporated. This can take up to 1 hour. Pour into a bowl and cool.

Mix the egg yolks with the cream, and add to the onions with plenty of pepper. Adjust the salt if necessary before pouring into the pastry case. Try to make sure that you fill the tart as high as you dare – depending on the juices from the onion, you may have a little of the custardy liquid left over – but do try to get it all in. Half-filled tarts are always disappointing.

Bake in a preheated oven, 180°C (350°F), Gas Mark 4, for 30–40 minutes or until lightly browned.

The pastry area has to remain cool, which is difficult in a busy kitchen despite the marble slabs.

Yet another stalwart of the Bibendum à la carte. It is not at all essential to purchase a Bresse chicken (they are not exactly on every supermarket shelf), although if one were moved to so do, one would be astonished by its extraordinarily fine flavour and a real texture that is so very much missing from everyday British roasters. However, there are some fine chickens available on the market now, if you search them out, with the 'Label Anglaise' brand being a particularly good example.

125g/4oz good butter, at room temperature
1.8kg/4lb free-range chicken
1 lemon
several sprigs of thyme or tarragon, or a mixture of the two
1 garlic clove, crushed
salt and pepper

SERVES 4

Roast poulet de Bresse with tarragon

Smear the butter with your hands all over the bird. Put the chicken in a roasting tin that will accommodate it with room to spare. Season liberally with salt and pepper and squeeze over the juice of the lemon. Put the herbs and garlic inside the cavity, together with the squeezed out lemon halves – this will add a fragrant lemony flavour to the finished dish.

Roast the chicken in a preheated oven, 230°C (450°F), Gas Mark 8, for 10–15 minutes. Baste, then turn the oven temperature down to 190°C (375°F), Gas Mark 5, and roast for a further 30–45 minutes with a further occasional basting. The bird should be golden brown all over with a crisp skin and have buttery, lemony juices of a nut-brown colour in the bottom of the tin.

Turn off the oven, leaving the door ajar, and leave the chicken to rest for at least 15 minutes before carving. This enables the flesh to relax gently, retaining the juices in the meat and ensuring easy, trouble-free carving and a moist bird.

Carve the bird to suit yourself; I like to do it in the roasting tin. I see no point in making a gravy in that old-fashioned English way with the roasting fat, flour and vegetable cooking water. With this roasting method, what you end up with in the tin is an amalgamation of butter, lemon juice and chicken juices. That's all. It is a perfect homogenisation of fats and liquids. All it needs is a light whisk or a stir, and you have the most wonderful 'gravy' imaginable. If you wish to add extra flavour, you can scoop the garlic and herbs out of the chicken cavity, stir them into the gravy and heat through; strain before serving.

A roast chicken before being delivered to the customer.

Another idea, popular with the Italians, is sometimes known as 'wet-roasting'. Pour some white wine or a little chicken stock, or both, or even just water around the bottom of the tin at the beginning of cooking. This will produce more of a sauce and can be enriched further to produce altogether different results. For example, you can add chopped tomatoes, diced bacon, cream, endless different herbs, mushrooms, spring vegetables, spices – particularly saffron and ginger – or anything else that you fancy.

For me, the simplest roast bird is the best, but it is useful to know how much further you can go when roasting a chicken.

Opposite: Waiters come to collect the food from the pass in the kitchen – always a tense area.
Top: A chicken fresh out of the oven, generously laced with tarragon. Above: Bresse chicken arrive, ready for plucking.

I sometimes think that there are as many recipes for steak au poivre as there are chefs who cook them. This particular one is the first I ever learnt to cook (at the same time and place where I learnt to make snail butter; La Normandie) and, I most ardently feel, is up there with the very best versions. Simplicity – and with particular care taken when preparing the two peppers and judicious seasoning – is the key, here.

2 tablespoons white peppercorns
2 tablespoons black peppercorns
4 fillet steaks, about 175g/6oz each
3 tablespoons olive oil
75g/3oz unsalted butter
2 good slugs of Cognac
2 tablespoons meat juices/glaze (optional)
salt

SERVES 4

Steak au poivre

Crush the peppercorns coarsely in a pestle and mortar or in a coffee grinder. Tip the pepper into a sieve and shake well until all remnants of powder have been dispersed. (This is very important because all the excess powder will cause the steaks to be far too hot.) Press the peppercorns into both sides of each steak with your fingers, pressing well with the heel of your hand. Only now season with salt because salting first will not allow the pepper to stick to the meat.

Heat the olive oil in a frying pan until hot. Put in the steaks and fry on one side thoroughly, but not on full heat, until a good thick crust has formed. Add 50g/2oz of the butter and allow to colour to nut-brown. Turn the steaks over, and finish cooking to suit your taste. Try to resist turning too often – the aim is to produce a good crusty coating on each surface. Baste with the buttery juices as you go. Remove the steaks to hot plates, add the Cognac to the pan and whisk together with the butter. It matters not whether the brandy ignites, but the alcohol must be boiled off. Scrape and stir together any gooey bits from the bottom of the pan and whisk in the final bit of butter. Give a final boil and pour over the steaks. Serve with chips and a green salad.

Steak au poivre – a Bibendum classic.

There was quite a good deal of controversy over the decision to include fish and chips on the menu at Bibendum when we first opened. I guess, more than anything else, it was the shock of seeing the inexpensive, traditional British take-away item charged at à la carte, Chelsea restaurant prices! But we use the finest cod (sustainable), haddock, plaice or, occasionally, when we can find them, small, whole monkfish tails fried on the bone. Be assured, when you see these latter beauties are 'frying tonight', take them.

oil, for deep-frying the fish
4 cod fillets, about 175g/6oz each
seasoned flour, for dusting

BATTER
200g/7oz plain flour
50g/2oz potato flour (fécule)
1 bottle of beer (300ml/½ pint)
1 egg yolk
25ml/1 fl oz oil
250ml/8fl oz milk
salt and pepper

CHIPS
4 large floury potatoes
groundnut oil, for deep-frying

SERVES 4

Fish and chips

To make the batter, blend all the ingredients together, sieve and leave to rest for 1 hour.

Depending on whether you like your chips thin or thick, cut the potatoes lengthwise into the appropriate thickness. Then wash under cold running water until the water is clear and rid of all the starch. Drain in a colander and leave to dry before frying.

In a suitable pan or an electric deep-fryer, heat the oil for the chips until it has reached 150°C (300°F). Do allow yourself plenty of oil as the more you have in the pan, the less the temperature will drop when the chips are down! Put in the chips – don't overcrowd – and fry for 6–7 minutes. Lift one out and check it. It should be soft right through. If not, then give them another minute or so. Lift them out and allow to drain. Increase the temperature of the oil for the chips to 185°C (360°F).

Previous pages: The preparation of steak au poivre involves a generous slug of Cognac. Opposite: One of our all time favourites, fish and chips. Beautiful fish, perfect batter and double fried chips – it can't get much better.

Meanwhile, heat the oil for deep-frying the fish to 180°C (350°F). Dip the cod in the seasoned flour, then immediately into the batter and deep-fry for 5–7 minutes, depending on the thickness of the fillets.

Fry the chips a second time between 30 seconds and 2 minutes. This time variance depends very much on the type of potato available at different times of the year. Certain potatoes just will not crisp, so ask your greengrocer which are best.

Serve the fish and chips with lemon, vinegar, watercress, tartare sauce, ketchup… or whatever you will.

Careful preparation, battering and frying of the fish is essential to make the deceptively simple dish perfect.

Without wishing to sound immodest, I have a feeling that when this luscious spoonful of palest yellow mashed potato first made an appearance (at Hilaire, in 1984), it was to herald an ongoing welter of further flavourings to the humble, creamed tuber. Some, how shall we say, should never have seen the light of day (sun-dried tomato, broccoli, and horseradish – this last is particularly silly as, once heated, horseradish looses almost all its necessary pungency). The origins of this saffron version were inspired by the most delicious crushing of saffron-imbued boiled potatoes, gently crushed with a fork into the soup juices from a particularly fine bouillabaisse, eaten in Marseilles. At its very best, naturally, when eaten with fish.

1kg/2lb floury potatoes, cut into chunks
a generous teaspoon of saffron threads
1 large garlic clove, finely chopped
200ml/7fl oz creamy milk
200ml/7fl oz virgin olive oil
Tabasco sauce, to taste
salt

SERVES 4

Saffron mashed potatoes

Boil the potatoes in fish stock or water with some salt. Heat together the saffron, garlic and milk, cover and infuse while the potatoes are boiling. Add the olive oil to the milk infusion and gently reheat. Drain and mash the potatoes – I think the best texture achieved is through a *mouli-légumes*. Put the potatoes in the bowl of an electric mixer, switch on and add the saffron mixture in a steady stream. Add Tabasco to taste and adjust the seasoning. Allow the purée to sit in a warm place for about 30 minutes so that the saffron flavour is fully developed.

Time is a controlling factor in a restaurant and its kitchen, as is the humour of the staff and the relationship between the front of house and the kitchen brigade.

The most important consideration when making this gorgeous ice cream is to be as brave as possible when making the caramel; an 'adult' caramel is how one intelligently opinionated cook so accurately once put it to me. At the moment when one might think that the caramel is possibly about to be burnt and ruined, is the time to add the cream to the pan. However, at this point, do beware of explosive spluttering or 'Attention aux éclabousures!' as the originator of this ice cream, the great Fredy Girardet once warned. A paler, safer coloured caramel will produce a pale and safe ice cream – and who would want that?

250g/8oz caster sugar
1 vanilla pod, spilt lengthwise and broken into small pieces
200ml/7fl oz double cream
350ml/12fl oz milk
8 egg yolks

SERVES 4

Caramel ice cream

Heat the sugar gently in a heavy-bottomed pan until melted. Do not stir during this time, though you might like to tilt the pan from time to time to help it on its way. Once it is completely melted and golden brown, add the vanilla pod and stir gently with a wooden spoon until the caramel is a deep mahogany colour. Wait a moment longer or until you think the caramel might smell slightly burnt, and then add the cream. Be careful of the eruption and quickly stir to quell the bubbles. Heat the milk and beat the egg yolks and mix together. Add to the caramel/cream mixture and cook gently until just below boiling point, stirring constantly but gently until the sauce has a consistency of thin cream. Whisk together, strain through a fine sieve into a cold bowl and leave to cool. When cold, turn into an ice cream maker and freeze according to the manufacturer's instructions.

Discussion is vital and the director's opinions have to be transmitted to the staff. All staff have to be well briefed about the ever-changing menu and wine list.

The origins of this rich little chocolate pastry hark back to the early 1980's, in south-west France, when I was generously taken by friends to have lunch chez Guerard, at his three star restaurant in Eugenie-les-Bains. It is based upon the traditional almond cream pithiviers, most famously offered in patisseries all over France during the days following Christmas up to twelfth night. After a splendid lunch, I felt I had to ask of the great chef how he had made it: 'Well, you know, almond cream, a little chocolate and some puff pastry.' 'Oui, chef,' I thought. 'How very helpful.' After much tentative work – including many failures – I felt I had finally cracked it. Over 21 years on, thankfully, it is still going strong.

PASTRY
250g/8oz strong plain flour
a pinch of salt
250g/8oz cold unsalted butter, cut into small pieces
juice of 1/2 lemon
150ml/1/4 pint iced water

CRÈME PÂTISSIÈRE
250ml/9 fl oz milk
1 vanilla pod, spilt lengthways
3 egg yolks
75g/3 oz caster sugar
25g/1 oz plain flour

CHOCOLATE MIXTURE
125g/4oz unsalted butter, softened
125g/4oz caster sugar
2 small eggs
125g/4oz ground almonds
50g/2oz cocoa powder
1/2 teaspoon dark rum
125g/4oz plain chocolate, chopped
beaten egg, to glaze
icing sugar, to dust

SERVES 4

Chocolate pithiviers

To make the pastry, sift the flour and salt together into a bowl and add the butter. Loosely mix, but don't blend the ingredients together in the normal way of pastry-making. Mix the lemon juice with the iced water and pour into the butter/flour mixture. With a metal spoon, gently mix together until a cohesive mass has formed. Turn onto a cool surface and shape into a thick rectangle.

Flour the work surface and gently roll the pastry into a rectangle measuring about 18 x 10cm/7 x 4 inches. Fold one third of the rectangle over towards the centre

Chocolate pithviers won't last long on the plate – one of the most popular puddings and difficult to make but well worth it.

and fold the remaining third over that. Lightly press together and rest the pastry in the fridge for 10 minutes.

Return the pastry to the same position on the work surface and turn it through 90 degrees. Roll it out to the same dimensions as before, and fold and rest again in the same way. Repeat this turning, rolling, folding and resting process three more times. (Phew! This is the moment when you wish you'd bought ready-made pastry.) Place the pastry in a polythene bag and leave in the fridge for several hours or overnight.

To make the crème pâtissière, put the milk in a saucepan with the vanilla pod and heat gently to boiling point. Whisk together the egg yolks, sugar and flour. Pour the hot milk onto the egg mixture and whisk lightly together. Return the mixture to the saucepan and cook gently until it thickens. Pour through a sieve, discard the vanilla pod and chill.

To make the chocolate mixture, cream the butter and sugar together until light and fluffy. Add the eggs and beat again. Now add the ground almonds and cocoa powder. Beat again. Add the rum together with the crème pâtissière and finally fold in the chopped chocolate. Chill.

Roll out the pastry to about 3mm/⅛ inch thick. Cut it into four 10cm/4 inch and four 15cm/6 inch squares. Place the smaller squares on a floured board. Using a large ice cream scoop, place a scoop of the chocolate mixture in the centre of each of the small squares of pastry. Brush the pastry edges with half the beaten egg, place the larger squares of pastry on top and press down and around firmly, making sure there are no air bubbles.

Use a 10cm/4 inch round pastry cutter to cut the filled pastry squares into neat rounds. Discard the trimmings. Press and seal together the edges with a fork to form a decorative pattern. Brush the pithiviers with the remaining beaten egg and dust lightly with icing sugar. Place on a greased baking sheet and bake in a preheated oven at 200°C (400°F), Gas Mark 6 for 15–20 minutes or until the pastry is well risen, shiny and golden brown. Remove from the oven, dust lightly with some more icing sugar, and serve hot with thick cream.

Preparation in the small service area in the Oyster Bar beneath one of the wonderful Michelin ceramic plaques depicting a Russian rally, circa 1908.

The Royal Borough of Kensington and Chelsea
SLOANE AVENUE SW3

In conversation: kitchen memories

What were your early influences and how did they feed into Bibendum?

Simon: Effectively supportive parents who both loved to cook and eat good food. But I knew I wanted to cook, ever since making my first mayonnaise, aged 13, in the house in which I grew up.

Jeremy: I ate dinner at Bibendum in the very early days and the simplicity and elegance of that cooking in equal measure had me beating a path to that kitchen door like a rocket. The combination of Simon's cooking eaten in that beautiful dining room in that remarkable building marvellously elevated such a great moment.

Are you cooks or chefs and why?

Jeremy: Terms like 'Chef' were never used, the preference being that cooks had names, personality and ability. Also, that extraordinary thing of being given the chance to write our own menus for the lunchtime service. Such opportunity is rare in the restaurant business and with the produce that arrived daily into that kitchen, such an opportunity was inspiring indeed.

Simon: Personally, I think I have always been a cook. Perseverance and passion, is all — cooks and chefs alike. One only ever wishes to please those who eat the food one has cooked.

How would you describe the experience of cooking at Bibendum?

Simon: In a word, busy. Frustrating, also, as I have never been particularly good at delegating. When those who eat in restaurants think that the chef cooks everything — and there are many foolish folk who do have exactly that thought — I have always wished that this were true. Which is an equally foolish state of mind!

Jeremy: Yes, it was a lot of hard work, nothing new there, but the kitchen crew were young and bright — there were no shrinking violets amongst those cooks, quite the reverse — I have many memories of much laughing and the occasional song being belted out!

Simon: I loved cooking lunches more than anything else. And preparation, butchery in particular. I often said that I would be quite happy to go home after lunch, everything prepared for the day and a buzzing lunch service over. And then not return for dinner!

Jeremy: The main course sections, MC1 and MC2, were always where I wanted to be. Watching the effortless cooking of perfect scallops, filet au poivre, cote de boeuf and of course, that marvellous roast chicken, a whole poulet de Bresse for two, my favourite dish. What were your favourites?

Simon: Escargots: large, succulent snails with a bubbling garlic butter still frothing when it reaches the table. Inspired by those served at the legendary Chez L'Ami Louis

Simon Hopkinson and Jeremy Lee under the ever watchful eye of Monsieur Bibendum.

restaurant, in Paris. And, I have to agree with you, that roast Bresse chicken: as simple and perfect as chicken can be; buttery, winy, tarragon flavoured and with crisp skin.

What is your fondest kitchen memory at Bibendum?

Simon: Cooking the late George Perry-Smith's dinner to celebrate his wedding to Heather Crosbie.

Jeremy: When starting a lunch service one day, there was a slight commotion at the lift and I looked up to see Elizabeth David being aided out of the lift in her wheelchair and gently taken to the dining room. I had just brought a lemon tart out of the oven which the great lady ate after her lunch and pronounced it the best she'd ever had. This memory is one that makes Bibendum very special for me.

Simon: One of my funniest memories was when we employed a charming French maitre d' called Pascal. One evening, the Duke and Duchess of York came to dinner. The Duchess arrived first and was directed to a nice corner table. Opposite, on the other side of the room, a smaller table was also reserved for two body guards. Pascal, not necessarily au fait with royal personages, moments later similarly directed a be-suited, smart young man to the bodyguard's table and managed to sit him down. Pascal noted that he looked somewhat perplexed. 'Is something wrong, sir?', Pascal enquired. The gentleman then asked that might he be allowed to sit with his wife…

Chefs such as Bruce Poole, Henry Harris and Philip Howard have all worked at Bibendum in the past and gone on to achieve acclaim in their own right. Do you think their time has influenced what they do now?

Simon: One would very much like to think so. Bruce, I think, may have taken the robustness and richness of some of the dishes Bibendum is well known for, whereas Henry possibly added his personal to his already good knowledge of French food.

Jeremy: Henry certainly ate and learnt a lot; he's since dazzled at Harvey Nichols but I think he has truly shone at Racine. Philip Howard also cooked a treat while at Bibendum dreaming of Michelin stars which he has now got.

Simon: Yes, Philip was always more of a Michelin man and now cooks food of the greatest finesse and style, earning himself two much deserved – and coveted – Michelin stars, in the process.

Jeremy: Did you offer any advice to Matthew Harris when he took over as Head Chef?

Simon: Well, not so much advice, more a suggestion that he might like to keep some of the most favourite dishes alive and well post my departure. There is something very important about familiarity on a menu, much appreciated by regular customers who sometimes choose not to eat anything else but that which they know and love. Matthew has firmly embraced this continuity and it is very touching to see how clearly important it is to him, too. When Matthew first worked for me at Hilaire [in 1984], it was obvious that here was someone with a keen love of good food. Together with this, and his strength of will and organisation, Matthew has continued to uphold all the fine traditions of a great working kitchen. He has worked at Bibendum for the last 21 years – and I salute him!

How do you think Bibendum stands up now, 21 years later?

Simon: A good restaurant is a combination of several qualities: comfort, an efficient and kindly service, good food, well chosen and carefully served drinks and wine, and a long standing, loyal staff. Terence's dining room design still looks wonderful today and the Oyster Bar and relatively newer Café continue to attract regulars and new clients alike. Considering quite how many restaurants there are now in London, compared with 1987, when we opened, I think we may have made a mark…

Simon and Jeremy chatting away. 81 Fulham Road is the entrance for the Café and Oyster Bar. The smell of sizzling snails is remeniscent of Paris.

JAMBON PERSILLE WITH SAUCE GRIBICHE

DEVILLED LAMBS' KIDNEYS ON TOAST

MARINATED SEA BASS WITH FENNEL, BLOOD ORANGES AND GREEN PEPPERCORNS

ASPARAGUS WITH MORELS AND POACHED EGGS

SAUTEED RABBIT WITH YOUNG GARLIC AND BASIL

ROAST BEST END OF LAMB WITH PITHIVIERS SAVOYARDE

GRILLED VEAL CHOP WITH ANCHOVY AND ROSEMARY BUTTER

ROAST QUAILS WITH WHITE WINE AND SAGE

CHAMPAGNE AND BLOOD ORANGE JELLIES WITH BUTTER CAKE

ICED ZABABLIONE PARFAIT

RUM BABAS WITH PINEAPPLE IN KIRSCH

PASSIONFRUIT TART

Spring

Recipes by Matthew Harris

The ceramic mosiac in the floor of the lobby depicts Monsieur Bibendum drinking nails, glass and flints with the caption 'Nunc est Bibendum' (now is the time to drink) – a very appropriate sub-text for our restaurant.

Jellied ham hock with parsley is a classic and best served with a creamy and sharp sauce like gribiche. It is such a shame that so many chefs feel it necessary to mess around with such a classic by adding such ingredients as foie gras or sweetbreads. It stands up on its own and should be left to do so.

2 ham hocks
2 pig's trotters (optional)
2 large carrots, cut into 4cm/1 ¾ inch chunks
2 onions, cut into 4cm/1 ¾ inch chunks
1 leek, cut into 4cm/1 ¾ inch chunks
4 sticks of celery, cut into 4cm/1 ¾ inch chunks
1 sprig of thyme
4 bay leaves
3 garlic cloves
1 teaspoon white peppercorns
50ml/2fl oz white wine vinegar
leaves from 2 bunches of flat-leaf parsley, chopped
¼ teaspoon grated nutmeg
12–14 leaves of gelatine, 2g each

SAUCE GRIBICHE
1 tablespoon capers, finely chopped
12 cornichons, finely chopped
2 hard-boiled eggs
3 egg yolks
1 tablespoon Dijon mustard
2 tablespoons red wine vinegar
300ml/½ pint groundnut oil
1 tablespoon chopped flat-leaf parsley
1 tablespoon chopped tarragon
salt and freshly ground black pepper

SERVES 6–10

Jambon persillé with sauce gribiche

Put the ham hocks, pig's trotters (if using), the vegetables, thyme, bay leaves, garlic, peppercorns and vinegar into a large saucepan and cover with water. Bring to the boil and then turn down to a simmer. After 20 minutes remove the scum that has risen to the surface with a ladle. Allow the hocks to simmer gently for 3–4 hours until cooked. You can tell when they are done because you will be able to pull out the small bone (next to the big bone) easily. Incidentally, in France this little bone is referred to as the mustard spoon due to its convenient shape.

Jambon persillé – delicious enough to tempt a vegetarian.

Remove the hocks and trotters if you are using them, (I do recommend using them as they will improve the flavour and also increase the gelatinousness of the stock, so less gelatine will need to be added at the end) and allow to cool to handling temperature.

Meanwhile, strain the cooking liquid through a fine sieve and discard the vegetables. Return the liquid to the stove. Remove any fat on the surface with a ladle and then bring the stock to the boil and allow it to reduce. You must be careful now because this will be the jelly so you must taste it regularly as it reduces, and when it is strong in flavour but not too salty remove it from the heat. If it gets too salty then add a little water until the salt level is to your liking. You will need 1 litre/1 3/4 pints of this stock to make the jelly; keep warm.

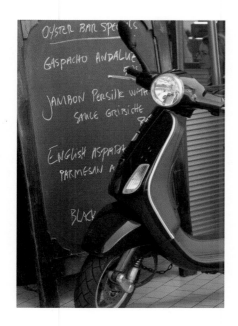

Return to the hocks and, with your hands, remove the skin and fat and put to one side. Now break up the pieces of meat into 3cm/1 1/4 inch bits. Pick through the trotters as well and you will get some little bits of meat from them, too. Put the ham pieces in a large bowl. If you like a bit of fat and skin then add a few small pieces, too. Add the parsley, nutmeg and a few twists of ground pepper.

Next, fill a 1.5kg terrine mould with the ham/parsley mixture but do not push it down, you need gaps for the jelly to get into. Set aside.

To make the jelly, if you have used trotters, 12 leaves of gelatine should be enough, if not use 14 leaves. Allow the gelatine leaves to soften in cold water then remove them and stir into the measured warm stock until completely dissolved. Pour this over the ham until the terrine is completely full. You may well have left-over jelly. Now refrigerate the jambon persillé overnight.

To make the sauce gribiche, first, place the capers and cornichons in a bowl. Into this grate the hard-boiled eggs, using the large holes on the grater. In another bowl, place the egg yolks, mustard and red wine vinegar and whisk until well mixed. Start adding the oil in a thin stream whilst continuing to whisk, as for mayonnaise. The oil will emulsify with the yolks producing a creamy mayonnaise. When all is added stir into the grated egg, the capers and cornichons. Add the herbs and season with salt and pepper. Refrigerate until ready to serve.

To serve, give a thick slice with a good spoonful of sauce gribiche and some toasted baguette.

A chef arriving for work in his Fiat – will he get out? Behind him, the flower shop in the lobby of the building. You can have lunch in the restaurant above and get flowers delivered to the girl of your dreams as you eat.

This would be equally good served as a hearty breakfast as it is a starter. At the restaurant we use toasted sourdough bread that we make ourselves from a 'starter' (rising agent used for sourdough breads) that is now several years old. However, if you can get it, toasted Poîlane bread would be a good substitute.

6 lambs' kidneys, fat removed
50g/2oz unsalted butter
2 tablespoons oil
100g/3½oz button mushrooms, thinly sliced
400g/14oz shallots, thinly sliced
1 teaspoon tomato purée
½ teaspoon cayenne pepper
½ teaspoon English mustard powder
4 tablespoons brandy
125ml/4fl oz strong jellied chicken stock, (see page 76)
4 teaspoons Worcestershire sauce
4 slices sourdough bread

KIDNEY SEASONING
½ teaspoon cayenne
½ teaspoon English mustard powder
2 tablespoons plain flour
salt and freshly ground black pepper

SERVES 4

Devilled lambs' kidneys on toast

To make the kidney seasoning, combine all the ingredients in a bowl and set aside.

Cut the kidneys in half lengthwise so you end up with two 'C' shaped pieces. Remove any remaining fat and the cores with a small knife, and put the kidneys to one side.

In a saucepan, heat the butter and oil then add the mushrooms and shallots and fry gently until golden. Add the tomato purée, the cayenne and mustard powder and fry for a further few minutes before adding the brandy. Allow the brandy to evaporate – be careful it might ignite – then add the stock and Worcestershire sauce. Let this simmer away and reduce for a few minutes until a rich glossy sauce is achieved. Season with salt and pepper and keep warm.

Toast the bread and keep warm. Heat a frying pan and add a little oil. Then dip the kidneys in the seasoning mix, thoroughly covering them. Shake off any excess and fry until crusty and brown then turn over and fry for a minute on the other side. This should leave them pink in the middle; cook for longer if you like them well done. To serve, give 1 slice of toast per person with three half kidneys on top and spoon over plenty of sauce.

A well trained, cheerful, dedicated staff are essential for a successful restaurant.

This makes a wonderfully light, sharp and somewhat spicy starter. When the Italian blood oranges are in full flow, their ruby flesh also makes a stunning visual contrast to the sea bass and fennel.

2 fennel bulbs
2 teaspoons olive oil, plus extra for drizzling
juice of 1/2 lemon
4 blood oranges
600g/1lb 2oz very fresh sea bass fillet, skin and bones removed
1 small jar of green peppercorns in brine, drained
100ml/3 1/2fl oz mayonnaise

SERVES 6

Marinated sea bass with fennel, blood oranges and green peppercorns

For this recipe you will need a mandolin to slice the fennel thin enough. The plastic Japanese ones are great for this, though they can be dangerous so watch your fingers! Thinly slice the fennel – it should be almost translucent – and then dress it with a few dribbles of olive oil and the lemon half squeezed over. Season with salt and toss. Put to one side.

Peel the zest of the oranges with a zester and blanch the strips in boiling water. Do this twice to remove any bitterness and then refresh in cold water. This julienne of orange zest will be used as a garnish.

Remove the pith and segment the oranges (see the method on page 124). Put the segments in a bowl to get some blood orange juice and squeeze out the orange cores to extract all the remaining juice. Add the lemon juice. Season with salt and pepper, add the olive oil and whisk briefly.

Now thinly slice the sea bass by cutting straight down – not angled like smoked salmon – 2mm/scant 1/8 inch thick is ideal. Marinate the sea bass in the orange juice mix for 5 minutes.

Meanwhile, in a pestle and mortar, crush 2 teaspoons of the drained green peppercorns to a paste and then mix in the mayonnaise.

You are now ready to serve. Spread out 6 serving plates and cover each with some loosely scattered fennel, then lay the strips of sea bass over this. You should have about 8 strips each. Next scatter the segments and the julienne of oranges and drizzle with a few blobs of the green peppercorn dressing. Finally, distribute a few of the remaining whole green peppercorns over each dish and serve.

The marinated sea bass starter is a perfect example of a well balanced dish that has the right combination of carefully considered flavours.

By May the English asparagus season is getting into full swing and so are fresh morels from France. These two ingredients served together and topped with a poached egg could easily make a one-course lunch or a comforting late supper dish.

200g/7oz fresh morels, or more if you have lots!
50g/2oz unsalted butter
1 garlic clove, finely chopped
50ml/2fl oz Madeira
200ml/7fl oz strong jellied chicken stock (see page 76)
20 asparagus spears
splash of white wine vinegar
4 large eggs
1 bunch of chives, finely chopped
salt and freshly ground black pepper

SERVES 4

Asparagus with morels and poached eggs

You will need a large pan of boiling salted water for the asparagus; put it on to boil.

Take particular care about the cleaning the morels as they are very delicate and halve any large ones. In a large frying pan, melt 25g/1oz of the butter and sauté the morels, seasoned with a little salt and pepper. After 2 minutes, add the garlic to the mushrooms. Stir around and then add the Madeira. Let this bubble and reduce by half before adding the chicken stock. Bring it to the boil and take away from the heat.

Cook the asparagus: 4–5 minutes for medium-large asparagus is plenty.

Meanwhile, put a wide shallow pan of water with a splash of white wine vinegar on to boil for the poached eggs. Adjust the heat so the liquid is simmering. Crack each egg in turn into a saucer then carefully slip the egg into the water to poach, taking care to leave the yolks runny; 2 minutes will suffice. Scoop out with a slotted spoon onto a wodge of kitchen paper to drain.

To serve, return the mushroom sauce to the heat and bring to the boil. Now whisk in the remaining butter and add the chopped chives.

Divide the asparagus among warm plates, with the tips all at the same end. On top place a poached egg and then spoon the morel sauce over. Serve with plenty of crusty bread.

The Oyster Bar where the specially designed chairs, tables and bar front all mirror the shape of Monsieur Bibendum's chubby curves.

Rabbit has long been a firm favourite at the restaurant. In this recipe only the legs and saddles are used, however, if you buy whole rabbits the shoulders can be used in a soup or a cassoulet.

2 French rabbits, heads and shoulders removed, saddle cut into 2, legs removed and separated
oil
4 heads new season's garlic, divided into unpeeled cloves
50g/2oz unsalted butter
250ml/8fl oz white wine
bunch of basil, chopped
salt and freshly ground black pepper

STRONG JELLIED CHICKEN STOCK (MAKES 2 LITRES/3½ PINTS)
2kg/4lb chicken carcasses
1 pig's trotter
200g/7oz each carrots, onions, leeks and celery, cut into 4cm/1¼ inch dice
100g/3½fl oz mushrooms, cut into 4-cm/1¼-inch dice
1 bunch of thyme
1 garlic head
6 bay leaves

SERVES 4

Sautéed rabbit with young garlic and basil

To make the chicken stock: place all the ingredients in a 12–15 litre/2½–3½ gallon saucepan and fill up with water. Bring to the boil then turn down to a simmer. Allow this to cook for 7–8 hours. Don't forget to skim off the fat and scum regularly and top up with water to keep the pan full. Once cooked, pass the stock through a fine conical strainer and return to the stove in a clean pan. Bring back to the boil and let it boil and reduce by two-thirds until you are left with a strong brown chicken stock. Allow to cool then refrigerate, or freeze in small containers for future use.

Ask your butcher to joint your rabbits if you don't care to do this. One thing you must do is remove the sinewy membrane on the outside of the saddle. Do this by inserting a sharp knife underneath and sliding it along to the other end, trying not to cut into the saddle meat. Season the saddles and legs and place in a large hot roasting tin on the hob and sauté in a little oil until golden all over. Then add the garlic and stir. Place in a preheated oven to 220°C (425°F), Gas Mark 7, for 20 minutes. Remove the rabbit and garlic from the pan, cover and keep warm.

Return the pan to the hob and add 25g/1oz of the butter and the white wine. With a whisk scrape away at the bottom and edge of the pan, getting all the crusty bits into the sauce. Reduce the wine by half then add 250ml/8fl oz of stock and reduce until you have a rich looking gravy. Whisk in the remaining butter to enrich the sauce. Add the basil, check for seasoning and pour over the rabbit and garlic.

Below right: Matthew Harris, head chef and king of all he surveys. Every detail in the kitchen is Matthew's responsibility which includes the quality of the raw ingredients and the food on the plate once it's been cooked.

There is something very satisfying about making a delicious meal out of leftovers. The leftover in this case is gratin dauphinois. You could of course make a gratin specifically for this dish. However, since the gratin has to be chilled before it is used why not make enough for two meals.

3 racks of lamb, plus chopped up bones from the best end
100g/3 1/2 oz carrot, chopped
100g/3 1/2 oz leek, chopped
100g/3 1/2 oz onion, chopped
100g/3 1/2 oz celery, chopped
100g/3 1/2 oz mushrooms, chopped
1/2 bottle red wine
1 sprig of thyme
1 garlic clove, crushed
1 teaspoon redcurrant jelly

PITHIVIERS SAVOYARDE
left-over gratin dauphinoise (for recipe see below)
125g/4oz grated Gruyère cheese
6 slices of air-dried ham or prosciutto
750g/1 1/2lb puff pastry
1 egg, beaten
1 egg yolk

GRATIN DAUPHINOIS
2kg/4lb potatoes
1 litre/1 3/4 pints double cream
5 garlic cloves, finely chopped
1 teaspoon chopped thyme

SERVES 6

Roast best end of lamb with pithiviers Savoyarde

To make the pithiviers, push a 3cm/1 1/4 inch pastry ring into the chilled gratin then pull it out and push out the round cylinder of gratin. Repeat 5 times. Place the grated Gruyère in a mixing bowl and, using your fingers, 1 cylinder at a time, cover them with Gruyère. Squash it on firmly and use your hand to form a cheese covered gratin ball. Completely cover each ball with a slice of ham, roll it around and squash the edges in. This is the filling; it should be about the size of a golf ball.

Roll out the puff pastry to 3mm/1/8 inch thick and cut out 6 discs that are 10cm/ 4 inches in diameter and another 6 discs that are 14cm/5 3/4 inches diameter. The smaller ones are the bases so lay these out on the work surface and put a ball of the filling in the centre of each one. Use a pastry brush to paint a circle of beaten egg around each ball on the pastry. Then lay the larger piece of pastry over the top

A perfect example of the Bibendum philosophy: a simple presentation of delicious but unpretentious food where the quality of the ingredients is paramount.

of the ball and push the edges down on to the smaller disc, creating a dome-shaped pie. Press the edges together firmly so they cannot leak. With the pastry brush paint the outside of the pithiviers with the egg yolk. This will give it a rich glaze when cooked. Refrigerate the pithiviers until you are ready to cook them.

To make gravy to go with the roast lamb, make sure the butcher gives you the chopped up bones from the best end. Spread these in a roasting tin and roast in a preheated oven, 200°C (400°F), Gas Mark 6, until golden then add the carrot, leek, onion, celery and mushrooms and allow these to roast with the bones until golden. Remove from the oven and scrape everything into a saucepan.

Pour the red wine into the roasting tin and scrape away any sticky bits. Pour into a saucepan, along with the thyme, garlic and redcurrant jelly. Top up the pan with water to the top of the bones and allow to gently simmer uncovered for at least 2 hours. Strain through a fine sieve and reduce the liquid to a rich, strong tasting gravy. Keep warm.

Season the best ends and roast in a preheated oven, 200°C (400°F), Gas Mark 6, for about 15–20 minutes depending on how well done you like them. Put the pithiviers in the oven 5 minutes before you take out the lamb; they will take 15 minutes to cook, allowing the lamb to rest somewhere warm.

To serve, slice the lamb into cutlets and serve with a pithiviers and some gravy.

GRATIN DAUPHINOIS (SERVES 6)

If you don't already have any left-over gratin dauphinois, try this classic recipe: take your favourite medium-sized oven-to-table dish and lightly butter it. Slice the potatoes 2mm/scant ⅛ inch thick on a mandolin. Pour the double cream into a bowl; add the garlic and thyme. Season with salt and pepper. Fill the dish on the bottom with slices of potato, overlapping slightly like roof tiles. When you have one layer of potato, cover with some cream. Continue layering and creaming the potatoes until you have a gratin about 3cm/1 ¼ inches deep. It seems like a lot of cream, but it is necessary. Cook in a preheated oven, 180°C (350°F), Gas Mark 4, for 50–60 minutes. Check that the potatoes are cooked with the point of a knife. The knife should go in like it was going through soft butter and is then ready to serve. You will only need half this amount to form the basis of the pithiviers Savoyarde. Leave it in the dish and chill overnight in the fridge.

Dedicated and careful work in the kitchen.

This compound butter is a firm favourite at the restaurant, served on a variety of different grilled meats and offal. I think however, that with a juicy, pink and tender veal chop it is simplicity at its best. This butter also freezes very well so could be made in bigger batches and used at will.

50g/2oz unsalted butter, softened to room temperature
grated rind of 1 lemon
1 teaspoon finely chopped rosemary
2 garlic cloves, finely chopped
75g/3oz drained anchovy fillets in oil, finely chopped
freshly ground black pepper
8 veal chops, about 275g/9oz each
8 lemon wedges, to serve

SERVES 8

Grilled veal chop with anchovy and rosemary butter

In a mixing bowl and using a spoon, mix the butter, lemon, rosemary and garlic together. Stir in the anchovies. Season with lots of freshly ground pepper. Now take a sheet of foil about 50cm/20 inches long and spoon the softened butter in blobs along the middle. Fold the top corners to the bottom so you have the beginnings of a roll. Roll it up tightly into a tube and twist the ends closed so the butter is moulded into a roll. Refrigerate for 2 hours or until firm.

Now cook the chops either in a preheated ribbed bottom pan or under a preheated char grill. Chops that are 2cm/³⁄4 inch thick will take about 4–5 minutes on each side. This will leave them pink in the middle. Now remove the chops from the grill. Peel off all the foil from the tube of butter and slice into 5mm/¹⁄4-inch thick discs. Put 1 or 2 discs on each chop and allow to rest somewhere warm for 5–8 minutes before serving with a wedge of lemon.

A delicious and simple dish of veal chop and anchovy butter. Very Bibendum.

Simply roasted plump quails cooked in butter are a quick and easy dish to prepare. With the addition of a few sage leaves and some white wine, a very simple yet impressive main course can be achieved.

125g/4oz unsalted butter
8 large quails
leaves from 1 bunch of sage
1 garlic clove, chopped
250ml/8fl oz white wine
200ml/7fl oz strong jellied chicken stock (see page 76)
salt and freshly ground black pepper

SERVES 4

Roast quails with white wine and sage

Soften half the butter and rub all over the quails, making sure they are covered. Season with salt and pepper and place in a roasting tin and roast in a preheated oven, 220°C (425°F), Gas Mark 7, for 25 minutes until golden all over. When cooked remove from the tin and keep them warm.

Now add the rest of the butter to the tin and put on the hob. Once the butter has melted and is sizzling add the sage leaves and fry until crisp. Remove and place on some kitchen paper and season with salt. If the butter starts to brown that is fine, but if it starts to burn turn the heat down.

As soon as the sage is removed add the garlic and fry for 15 seconds before adding the wine. Allow this to reduce by two-thirds and then add the stock. Bring to the boil, whisk everything together and allow the sauce to reduce until a shiny emulsified sauce is achieved. Taste the sauce and season with more salt, if necessary.

To serve, place two quails on each plate. Cover with a couple of spoonfuls of sauce and top with some of the crisp sage leaves.

Previous pages: A veal chop being grilled. Opposite: Waiters are briefed on the menu before a service. Chair covers for the autumn season being delivered – the colours are changed four times a year to reflect the seasons.

This is really grown up nursery food. Warm rich moist and buttery sponge, whipped cream and jelly plus, of course, Champagne for the adults!

BUTTER CAKES

7 egg yolks
175g/6oz caster sugar
100g/3 1/2oz potato flour (fécule)
10g/1/2oz plain flour
175g/6oz unsalted butter, melted

CHAMPAGNE AND BLOOD ORANGE JELLIES

3 blood oranges
1/2 bottle Champagne
2 tablespoons Grand Marnier
75g/3oz caster sugar
4 gelatine leaves
1/2 recipe Crème Chantilly (see page 94)

SERVES 4–6

Champagne and blood orange jellies with butter cake

The butter cake works best if the mix is made a day before cooking and refrigerated. Whisk the yolks and sugar in a food mixer for 20 minutes. Then sieve the potato flour and plain flour together and fold in. Next, stir in the melted butter until fully incorporated. Rest in the fridge overnight.

To make the jellies, peel and segment the oranges using the method on page 124. Distribute the segments evenly into ramekins, filling them about half way. Soak the gelatine in cold water until softened. Warm the Champagne and Grand Marnier with the sugar until the sugar is dissolved. Remove from the heat. Take the softened gelatine leaves out of the water and stir into the Champagne until dissolved. Now fill the ramekins with the jelly mix and put in the fridge to set.

To bake the cakes, cut out 4–6 strips of baking parchment to line the inside of individual cake rings 4cm/1 3/4 inches high and 4cm/1 3/4 inches in diameter. Place the rings on a baking sheet that is covered with another piece of baking parchment. Using a small spoon half fill the cake rings with the cake mixture and bake in a preheated oven, 170°C (335°F), Gas Mark 3 1/2 for 12–15 minutes or until golden on top. Remove from the oven and unmould them onto a wire rack. Keep warm.

To serve, very briefly dip the bottoms of the ramekins in hot water and then invert the jellies onto plates. Add a cake and a spoonful of crème chantilly.

A really important part of the restaurant is the briefing of the front of house staff by the kitchen and the wine buyer. Sometimes they have heard it all before and are rather bored by the repetition.

This is a great frozen dessert to make because it does not require an ice cream machine.

1 recipe Sponge Cake, without the Amaretto liqueur (see page 218)
375g/12oz caster sugar
9 egg yolks
150ml/¼ pint marsala
3 egg whites
400ml/14fl oz double cream
125g/4oz flaked almonds

CHOCOLATE SAUCE
150g/5oz cocoa powder, plus extra for dusting
400g/13oz caster sugar
600ml/1 pint water
60g/2½oz unsalted butter

SERVES 8–12

Iced zabaglione parfait

Using a cutter, cut circles from the sponge to fit the tops of 6.5cm (diameter) x 4cm-high individual cake rings. Place 125g/ 4oz of the sugar and 5 tablespoons water in a heavy-bottomed saucepan. Heat gently until the sugar has dissolved then cook until the temperature reaches 121°C/ 250°F on a sugar thermometer. If you don't have a thermometer, take a teaspoonful of the syrup and pour it into a cup of cold water – when you roll the syrup under the water, it should form a firm ball. Whilst the sugar is cooking, place the egg yolks in a food mixer and whisk until you have a thick and creamy sabayon. When the sugar is ready pour it in a thin steady stream into the yolks while the machine is running. Whisk for 5–10 minutes or until the sabayon has cooled. Whisk in the marsala and set aside. Next, heat 125g/ 4oz sugar with another 5 tablespoons water to 121°C/250°F. Place the egg whites in a clean food mixer bowl and whisk for 5 minutes or until white and fluffy. Whilst the machine is still running pour the sugar in a thin, steady stream as you did previously. Whisk for 5 more minutes and set aside.

Whisk the cream to ribbon stage so it is airy and slightly pourable. In a large bowl, fold the 2 egg mixtures together, retaining as much air as possible, then fold in the cream. Pour the mixture into the moulds and top each one with a sponge disc. Freeze overnight.

To make the chocolate sauce, place all the ingredients in a saucepan and gently bring up to the boil. Stir and simmer for 3 minutes then allow to cool. To make the praline crust, put the almonds and remaining 125g/4oz sugar in a saucepan over a medium heat. Stir with a wooden spoon until a rich brown caramel is achieved. Then pour onto a metal tray and allow it to cool. Once it is brittle break into pieces, put into a food processor and chop into a rough powder. When the parfaits are frozen, turn out upside down (so the sponge is the base), roll the edges in the praline powder and finish with a dusting of cocoa powder on top. Serve with chocolate sauce.

Previous pages: Preparation of the butter cakes to go with the Champagne and blood orange jellies.
Opposite: A delicious zabaglione parfait – very good at the end of a meal.

This is a very traditional dessert that I first learnt how to make when I was at l'Ecole Lenôtre pâtisserie school in Paris. Since then it has frequently found its way onto the menu. The combination of sweet, alcoholic soaked sponge with whipped cream and pineapple is a triumph.

100ml/3 1/2fl oz milk
7g/1/4oz fresh yeast or 1 1/2 teaspoons instant dried yeast
250g/8oz plain flour
1 tablespoon caster sugar
3 eggs, beaten
75g/3oz unsalted butter, softened
salt

RUM SYRUP
250g/8oz caster sugar
1/2 vanilla pod, split
grated zest of 1/2 lemon
1 large bay leaf
50ml/2fl oz dark rum

PINEAPPLE IN KIRSCH
250g/8oz caster sugar
1/2 vanilla pod, split
grated zest of 1/2 lemon
1 large bay leaf
50ml/2fl oz kirsch
1 pineapple, cut into 1–2cm/1/4 –3/4 inch slices

CRÈME CHANTILLY
250ml/8fl oz double cream
1 teaspoon vanilla essence
50g/2oz icing sugar

MAKES 5–7 BABAS

Rum babas with pineapple in kirsch

Warm the milk to blood temperature. Pour half into a bowl, add the fresh yeast, if using, and cream the two together and leave until dissolved. Add the flour, sugar and eggs and knead to a dough. If using instant dried yeast, simply stir it into the flour mixture. Add the rest of the milk (or all, if using instant dried yeast) and place in a food mixer with a paddle or dough hook and mix until smooth and it has become slightly elastic. Alternatively, turn the dough onto a floured work surface and knead by hand. Mix in the salt and butter, 1–2 knobs at a time until it is all incorporated. Now cover the mixing bowl with a tea towel and leave somewhere warm to prove until the dough is double in size. This can take up to 1 hour, sometimes a bit more. While the dough is proving, take 5–7 dariole moulds (non-stick are best) and rub butter around the

Simon, Matthew or Terence would not be a particularly tempting dish in the Oyster Bar but they are the major influences on the food Bibendum serves and its appearence.

Bibendum
Terence Conran
Simon Hopkinson
Matthew Harris
Roast rump of Lamb

insides, completely covering them. Dust the insides with flour. When the dough is ready, take a wooden spoon to it and stir vigorously, knocking out the air. Place it in a piping bag fitted with a large plain nozzle and pipe the dough into the dariole moulds, filling them half way up. Cover the moulds with a tea towel and leave somewhere warm to prove again. The dough should rise to near the top of the moulds, taking around 45 minutes. When risen, bake in a preheated oven, 180°C (350°F), Gas Mark 4, for 25 minutes or until golden on top. Take them out of their moulds and place them on a cooling rack.

To make the rum syrup, put the sugar, split vanilla pod, lemon zest, bay leaf and 250ml/8fl oz water into a saucepan. Bring to the boil, stirring, then remove from the heat and add the rum. Now drop the babas into the syrup, in batches, if necessary. They will float so keep turning them over gently and they will soak up the syrup. When they are soaked all the way through place them back on the cooling rack with a tray under it to catch any excess syrup. Refrigerate until ready to use.

To make the pineapples in kirsch, put the sugar, split vanilla pod, lemon zest, bay leaf and 250ml/8fl oz water into a saucepan. Bring to the boil, remove from the heat and add the kirsch. Using a pastry cutter just smaller then the pineapple slices, cut out the flesh and discard the skin. Cut out the core with a smaller cutter. Repeat this with 5–7 pineapple rings. Reheat the kirsch syrup to boiling again and add the pineapple rings. Turn off the heat and allow the pineapple to cool in the syrup. Refrigerate.

To make the crème chantilly, whip all the ingredients together until thick. Put in the fridge to chill before serving.

To serve, place one baba on each plate with a slice of pineapple and a spoonful of the syrup plus a large spoonful of crème chantilly.

Above: Matthew Harris, the head chef, and Simon Hopkinson, the original chef, confer and discuss menus and the general performance of the restaurant. Opposite: Don't know what the dog is doing, it certainly isn't on the menu.

A super smooth creamy tart with the real zingy punch of passionfruit. One slice of this ambrosial dessert is often not enough!

SWEET PASTRY
250g/8oz plain flour
pinch of salt
100g/3¹/₂oz icing sugar
100g/3¹/₂oz cold butter, diced
2 eggs, beaten

FILLING
about 30 passionfruit (see method)
7 large eggs, beaten
200g/7oz caster sugar
225ml/7¹/₂ fl oz double cream

SERVES 8

Passionfruit tart

To make the pastry, sieve together the flour, salt and sugar into a large bowl, add the butter and, with your hands, rub the butter into the flour/sugar until it is incorporated and no longer visible as butter. Then add the eggs and work into a soft but not sticky dough. Form into a ball, cover and chill for 2 hours.

Now, on a lightly floured surface and using a lightly floured rolling pin, roll out the pastry to a circle no more than 3mm/¹/₈ inch thick. Use to line a 26 x 2.5cm/ 10¹/₂ x 1 inch tart ring with a removable base. Make sure that there are no holes in the pastry case or it will leak when you add the filling. Having lined your pastry tin leave it to rest in the refrigerator for 30 minutes before blind baking: line the case with greaseproof paper and fill with baking beans. Cook at 180°C (350°F) Gas Mark 4 for 15–20 minutes until the base is pale golden. Remove the beans and paper and put the case to one side to cool slightly.

To make the filling, cut the passionfruit in half and scrape the pips and pulp into a fine sieve. Press with the back of a ladle or spoon to extract all the juice. Measure out 500ml/17fl oz passionfruit juice and mix with the eggs and sugar until completely smooth. Stir in the cream. Allow the mixture to sit for 5 minutes to allow any froth to rise to the surface; remove this with a spoon. Now pour the passionfruit mixture into the tart case and cook in the oven at 170°C (340°F) Gas Mark 3¹/₂ for 45 minutes until set. Allow to cool before serving.

Opposite and following pages: Preparation and presentation of passionfruit tart, one of our most delicious puddings. Light, elegant and unusual.

BY MATTHEW JUKES, WINE BUYER

Bibendum's wine list philosophy

My introduction to Bibendum Restaurant was, by anyone's standards, rather beguiling. The incredible building was daunting enough but it was the job that I was sent there to do which was a little scarier at the time. Back in 1990 I spent a few months selling Champagne to London's top restaurants and Bibendum's fame was such that every wine merchant wanted their wines on the wine list. I showed a rosé Champagne to the Bibendum general manager, who made me taste it blind against his own equivalent wine. We both agreed mine was the winner, but he didn't agree to list it, because

when I tried to close the sale, the tables were turned in the most unexpected way. He offered me a job on the spot – to compile a world-class wine list for Bibendum. I was totally flabbergasted. Of course I accepted and started that week. The aura surrounding the dining room, the stained glass windows, the design, the staff, the kitchen and in particular, Simon Hopkinson was fascinating and electrifying. The wine list at the time was a little stale, groaning with ancient classics, and it needed a spring clean. I set about my job with more energy than I had ever mustered before. I attended hundreds of wine tastings and within months understood intimately the machinations of the UK wine trade. During this time I got to know the menus in the Restaurant and the Oyster Bar, too – this was a very pleasurable part of my job. I also analyzed the sales of our wines very carefully indeed. It appeared to me that the Bibendum palate (I visualized M. Bibendum himself as our perfect restaurant customer in my brain when tasting, and I still do the same) was educated, 'classic', but adventurous if

given enough reason from our sommeliers. So, I started to augment the Italy, Spain, Australia and New Zealand chapters of the list – these countries were, and still are, making truly world class wines (at great value). Our reputation as the champions of groundbreaking new estates around the world was cemented. Within a year the *Good Food Guide* announced us the proud owners of the top wine list in the country with the excellent accolade: 'undoubtedly one of the finest wine lists in the country' and 'one of the most enthralling wine lists in the capital.' In 2003, The Carlton London Restaurant Awards gave us a gong for 'Most Exceptional Restaurant Wine List'.

Our team was very strong. François Vérité was a waiter back in 1990, but he fast became head sommelier. He is still with us. Richard Irmiger, a strong force in the wine team is still at Bibendum and working as a maitre d'. Countless wine waiters have

A fine wine list has always been Bibendum's ambition and together with the sommeliers and Matthew, the wine buyer, Bibendum has received recognition for their success.

been and gone, but a hearty band of them still keep in touch and I see many of the Aussies when touring Australia, tasting, and most of them own or manage their own restaurants. Bibendum has always been a breeding ground for fantastic chefs, but people often forget the wine academy side of things. We have had immense fun over the years and always make sure that every new wine is tasted by the wine waiters – a very rare occurrence in restaurants these days.

After working for Bibendum for eight years, I branched out and began a broadcasting career and started writing, while still managing the wines for Bibendum. Since then I have written ten wine books as well as a weekly column for a national newspaper. This privileged position means that I can travel the world in search of new and fascinating wines. On every trip Monsieur Bibendum is at my side. I often arrange for small parcels of wine to be shipped to the UK and we stock a large range of totally exclusive wines. We have always tried to be unique, so that our regular customers see an ever-evolving selection of wines. Bibendum's restaurant wine list is the only one in the UK that is updated every single week. With this in mind I have 'written' just under 1,000 wine lists for this incredible temple to gastronomy.

Our wine list fast became the touchstone for all enthusiastic young wine buyers, too. After all, back in 1990 not one restaurant in London had a dedicated wine buyer; most had a wine waiter who tried to squeeze list-compiling into breaks in their shifts. This inspirational move, thanks to the management, put us so far ahead of the competition that famous characters in the wine world always make a point of stopping by Michelin House on their own world tours. The most famous wine hero to cross the threshold was the great Henri Jayer, based in Vosne-Romanée, in Burgundy, and the godfather of red winemaking for the international wine industry. I had dinner with him many years ago and I remember him and his wife ordering the Lobster Club Sandwich as a starter and drinking with it some Coche-Dury, Meursault. This was the ultimate food and wine matching moment of my life. It was my great pleasure to offer them both a glass of 1811 Chabaneau Cognac after dinner. This was from a magnum that was discovered, buried in the cellar at Chabaneau by the new owners of the company, Camus. Not only was this wine the oldest I had ever tasted, but it was also from the celebrated vintage of the Great Comet, which was visible for nine months, and was in the sky when these grapes would have been on the vine. Henri declared it the greatest 'nose' he had ever encountered. This happened at Bibendum, and for a wine lover and someone who has dedicated himself to this great drink, it couldn't really have happened anywhere else.

The modern history of Bibendum's wine list continues with no changes whatsoever, and I intend to continue teaching young wine waiters our way of recommending, serving and wine and food matching. I also continue to update the list every week, stocking ever-more incredible wines from some of the rarest, greatest, newest and most cutting-edge wineries on the planet. It is what we do.

Just like food, wine and spirits have to be carefully briefed to the sommeliers. Sadly cigar training is no longer necessary – Monsieur Bibendum would be devastated.

TARTARE OF SALMON

SPICED ARTICHOKE SALAD

CEVICHE OF OYSTERS WITH CUCUMBER AND DILL

GRILLED CHICKEN LIVERS WITH PARSLEY SALAD AND GARLIC DRESSING

BREAST OF CHICKEN WITH PROSCIUTTO, HERBS AND CRUSHED JERSEY ROYALS

ROAST PIGEON WITH BRAISED LITTLE GEMS, PEAS AND MINT

BOILED LOBSTER WITH BROAD BEAN PUREE, LEMON AND CAPER VINAIGRETTE

FILLET OF WILD SALMON WITH SAUCE VIERGE

STRAWBERRY CHEESECAKE

GOOSEBERRY AND ELDERFLOWER FOOL

WATERMELON AND MINT GRANITA

ROAST PEACHES WITH RICOTTA, ALMONDS AND PORT

Summer

Recipes by Matthew Harris

One of the chefs pretending to look like Monsieur Bibendum having a good read of the menu.

We have been serving this version of salmon tartare since the restaurant opened and we still serve it the same way. Of course, it is important to have spanking fresh salmon and crisp freshly toasted baguette.

800g/1lb 6oz fresh salmon fillet, without skin
100g/3½oz anchovy fillets in oil, drained
4 egg yolks
150ml/¼ pint olive oil
2 tablespoons green peppercorns
1 tablespoon Worcestershire sauce
4 shakes of Tabasco sauce
4 cornichons
10 capers
4 large shallots, finely chopped
1 bunch of dill, finely chopped
8 teaspoons crème fraîche
salt and freshly ground black pepper
'keta' salmon caviar, to serve (optional)

SERVES 8

Tartare of salmon

Finely chop the salmon by hand and place in a large mixing bowl.

In a food processor, blend the anchovy fillets, egg yolks, olive oil, green peppercorns, Worcestershire sauce, Tabasco sauce, cornichons and capers to a smooth sauce. Spoon 6 tablespoonfuls onto the salmon. Add the shallot and dill then mix with a spoon. Season with salt and pepper.

Serve on individual plates with a teaspoon of crème fraîche on each one, and with a little caviar on top if desired. Serve with baguette, thinly sliced and toasted.

Any leftover sauce will keep in a sealed jar in the refrigerator for up to five days.

A delicious salmon starter for the summer months.

This North African-inspired salad with some buffalo mozzarella makes a very aromatic and satisfying starter when served at room temperature.

6 globe artichokes
1 lemon, halved
1 pinch of saffron strands
100ml/3 1/2fl oz olive oil
1 large onion, thinly sliced
1 teaspoon ground cumin
1 teaspoon ground allspice
2 garlic cloves, chopped
1 small chilli, seeds removed, chopped
2 tablespoons currants
4 tomatoes, skinned, deseeded and cut into strips
1 tablespoon mint, chopped
1 tablespoon parsley, chopped

SERVES 4

Spiced artichoke salad

Firstly, the artichokes need to be prepared and cooked. Hold the artichoke by the stalk and using a large serrated knife, cut the top half of the artichoke off. Now cut the stalk off. You will be left with the heart of the artichoke; the edges will still be covered with green leaves. These need to be removed so take a small sharp knife and trim these away until only the heart and choke remain. Squeeze the lemon into boiling salted water and simmer the heart and choke in this for 15–20 minutes. Check them by inserting a small sharp knife; it should go straight in like a cooked potato.

Allow the artichokes to cool, then use your fingers to remove and discard the choke. Cut the remaining saucer shaped hearts into 1-cm/1/2-inch cubes and put to one side.

Infuse the saffron in 100ml/3 1/2fl oz hot water.

Now in a large roomy saucepan heat the oil and sweat the onion until soft. Then add the cumin and allspice and fry for a further 3–4 minutes before adding the garlic and chilli. Fry briefly. Then add the artichokes, saffron and water, and currants. Stir over the heat for 2–3 minutes to allow the flavours to marry. Remove from the heat and leave to cool.

Before serving, add the tomatoes and chopped herbs.

Matthew tells Simon his best kitchen joke. Below, the counter in the Café, which sells delicious bridge rolls, paninis, hot salt beef sandwiches, salads and excellent coffee.

This is a delicious alternative to serving plain oysters on the half shell. The crunch of the cucumber and kick of the chilli really jazz them up.

1 cucumber
2 birds eye chillies, deseeded, finely diced
1 red onion, cut into (2.5mm/⅛ inch) dice
juice of 3 limes
1 bunch of dill, chopped
1 tablespoon olive oil
24 rock oysters
4 teaspoons crème fraîche
salt and freshly ground black pepper

SERVES 4

Ceviche of oysters with cucumber and dill

Peel the cucumber, then cut it in half lengthwise and remove the seeds with a teaspoon. Now cut the remaining flesh into fine dice (2.5mm/⅛ inch).

Mix together the chillies, red onion, lime juice, chopped dill, olive oil, and salt and pepper. Leave to marinate for 5 minutes in the refrigerator.

Whilst this is marinating, open the oysters. Spoon a heaped teaspoon of the mixture onto each oyster and allow to sit for 10 minutes before serving.

When serving, top each oyster with a small blob of crème fraîche.

Oysters are a great speciality of Bibendum both in the Restaurant and the Bar. We take great trouble with the supply and selection and have a close relationship with our suppliers.

I remember that years ago Simon Hopkinson went on holiday to Australia and he came back raving about a parsley salad he had whilst there. The ingredients were parsley leaves, anchovies, olives and onions and they were lovely. As recipes sometimes do over the years, it has developed and now I serve it as follows.

500g/1 lb chicken livers

PARSLEY SALAD
50g/2oz pitted black olives, chopped into quarters
50g/2oz flat-leaf parsley
50g/2oz finely chopped red onion
2 teaspoons small capers
1 garlic clove, finely chopped
10 anchovy fillets in oil, drained and chopped
grated zest of 1 lemon
100ml/3 ½fl oz extra virgin olive oil
juice of ½ lemon

GARLIC DRESSING
2 garlic cloves, finely chopped
juice of 1 lemon
2 egg yolks
1 teaspoon Dijon mustard
200ml/7fl oz extra virgin olive oil
salt and freshly ground black pepper

SERVES 4

Grilled chicken livers with parsley salad and garlic dressing

To make the parsley salad, mix everything together in a large bowl. Season with pepper and put to one side.

Next make the garlic dressing, which is essentially runny aioli. Whisk the garlic, lemon juice, egg yolks and Dijon mustard in a large bowl until well mixed and frothy. Now whisk in the olive oil in a thin stream as if making mayonnaise, taking care that it stays emulsified. If it looks as though it is starting to separate, add a splash of water and whisk that in before continuing with the oil.

When all the oil is added, whisk in some water to make it runny. It should be the consistency of salad cream. Season with salt and pepper and put to one side.

Simple inexpensive dishes like this chicken liver salad are an important part of the Oyster Bar menu – ideal for a quick lunch.

Put the chicken livers in a bowl and look through them to check there are no stringy white bits. If there are, cut them off with a small knife.

Heat a griddle pan or a frying pan, season the livers with salt and pepper and drizzle with a splash of oil to stop them sticking. Cook for a couple of minutes on each side, leaving a pink rosy blush in the middle. Cut one open to check if you are unsure.

To serve, place a good mound of the parsley salad on to each of 4 plates. Then distribute the livers evenly and finish the dish off with 1–2 tablespoons of drizzled garlic dressing.

Washing and drying the plates and kitchenware is a demanding but essential part of the life of every restaurant and café. Plates and glasses have to shine and the chefs are pretty demanding about their pots and pans.

This simple main course makes the ubiquitous chicken breast far more interesting. Serve with crushed Jersey Royals that soak up the herby butter that oozes from the chicken.

4 corn-fed chicken breasts, skinned
8 slices of prosciutto
400g/13oz Jersey Royal new potatoes
50g/2oz unsalted butter
4 spring onions, chopped
oil, for cooking the chicken
salt and freshly ground black pepper

HERB BUTTER
100g/3½fl oz unsalted butter
1 tablespoon chopped basil
1 tablespoon chopped tarragon
2 tablespoons chopped parsley
1 garlic clove, finely chopped
grated rind of 1 lemon

SERVES 4

Breast of chicken with prosciutto, herbs and crushed Jersey Royals

First, make the herb butter; in a large bowl soften the butter with your fingers, add the herbs and mix. Now mix in the garlic and lemon zest. Season with salt and pepper. Now mould the butter into the shape of 4 finger-size lozenges 5cm/2 inches long. Put these in the freezer for 30 minutes, to firm up.

Take the chicken breasts and using a small (7.5-cm/3-inch) thin, sharp kitchen knife, insert it in the rounded end of the breast at the edge where the wing was attached. Push it in about 6cm/2½ inches and wiggle it around a bit to make a pocket for the butter. Be careful not to puncture the breast with the tip of the knife. Remove the knife, insert the butter and squeeze the entrance hole together with your fingers. Then lay 2 slices of prosciutto side by side with the edges slightly overlapping, place the breast in the middle and wrap it up taking care to tuck the ends in. Repeat this process with the other breasts and then refrigerate for 1 hour to firm up.

Boil the potatoes in salted water until cooked. Drain and return to the pan with the butter, spring onions and salt and pepper. Crush lightly with the back of a fork or a potato masher. Keep warm.

To cook the chicken, pan-fry in a non-stick pan in a little oil until golden and a little crispy on both sides. About 4–5 minutes each side will suffice. Then finish in a preheated oven, 190°C (375°F), Gas Mark 5, for 10 minutes. Serve a nice scoop of the potato with the breast on top.

Clockwise from top right: Daily specials beautifully written on blackboards in the Café; clean aprons for waiting staff; cartoons of the French motoring fraternity circa 1900 decorate the walls of the restaurant; front of house.

BIBENDUM COFFEE BAR
TAKE AWAY PRICES

Espresso 1·60 Large 2·00
Cappuccino 1·80 Large 2·20
Latte 1·80 Large 2·20
Americano 1·60 Large 2·00
Hot chocolate 2·40 Tea/tisane 1·4
Croissant 1·80 Citronnier 2·
Pain au Chocolat 2·20 Muffins
Pain au raisin 2·20 2·40
lemon mascarpone danish 3·2

Anjou pigeon or squab are what I like to use here. Their juicy, tender breasts when served pink are a perfect accompaniment to the braised lettuce. It is certainly best to cook this dish when peas have just come into season and are at their smallest and sweetest.

groundnut or vegetable oil
2 x 450g/14–15oz pigeons
15g/¹/₂oz unsalted butter
50g/2oz pancetta, cut into thin strips 3mm/¹/₈ inch wide
2 Little Gem lettuce, halved lenthways
100ml/3¹/₂fl oz Madeira
200ml/7fl oz strong jellied chicken stock (see page 76)
100g/3¹/₂oz podded peas
1 tsp mint, chopped
salt and freshly ground black pepper

SERVES 2

Roast pigeon with braised little gems, peas and mint

In a large frying pan, heat a little oil. Season the pigeons and fry them whole to colour the breasts. This should take 2–3 minutes. Then roast them in a preheated oven, 240°C (475°F), Gas Mark 9 for 12 minutes. Remove them from the oven and leave somewhere warm to rest for 15 minutes.

Melt the butter in a wide saucepan and gently fry the pancetta until lightly coloured.

Rinse the lettuces briefly under the tap and shake dry. Now add the lettuce to the saucepan and fry for a few minutes, enough to colour the cut side of the lettuce. Add the Madeira, turn up the heat and bring to the boil. Allow this to reduce by two-thirds, and then add the stock. Bring to the boil and allow it to start reducing. Keep turning the lettuce over at frequent intervals to allow it to cook evenly. Add the peas and let them cook in the reducing liquid for 5–7 minutes. Keep tasting the sauce as it reduces and season with salt and pepper as necessary. When it has a glossy finish stir in the mint.

To serve, carve the pigeon off each carcass in two pieces, leaving the legs attached to the breast. Now put the lettuce halves in the centre of a plate and place the pigeon around it. Spoon the sauce and peas over and serve.

The plain white, blue banded china provides the ideal frame for food.

The best lobsters, I think, are native lobsters from the Dorset coast. Every summer at the restaurant we get through thousands of them. Although available at other times of the year they are most affordable in the summer months when they are in their prime. The amount of broad beans you need to buy will vary according to when in the summer you make this recipe. At the beginning of summer there are not very many in a pod while towards the end the pods are fuller and have bigger beans in them. It's better to buy too many and any spare are delicious tossed through a green salad and served on the side. The effort involved in podding and peeling the broad beans is well worth it. The richness of the purée with the juicy lobster and sharp vinaigrette is marvellous.

4 x 500 g/1 lb live lobsters
salt and freshly ground black pepper

LEMON AND CAPER VINAIGRETTE
2 lemons
4 shallots, finely chopped
2 tablespoons baby capers
4 tablespoons olive oil
2 tablespoons finely chopped flat-leaf parsley

BROAD BEAN PURÉE
1.5kg/3 lb podded broad beans
1 garlic clove
150ml/¼ pint olive oil

SERVES 4

Boiled lobster with broad bean purée, and lemon and caper vinaigrette

To make the lemon and caper vinaigrette, grate the lemon zest into a bowl and then peel all the pith from the lemons with a small knife. Now, carefully remove the flesh of each lemon by cutting in between the membrane that holds the lemon together, cutting towards the centre of the lemon. Do this each side of the membrane and the lemon flesh will drop out. Discard any pips from the flesh and add it to the zest. Now add the rest of the vinaigrette ingredients and mix; season with salt and pepper. Put to one side.

To make the broad bean purée, cook the beans in a large pan of boiling water for 30 seconds. Now drain and cool them either under running cold water or in a bowl of iced water. When cold, remove the outside skin of each bean by slitting the grey outside skin with your nail and popping out the green bean inside. This is the laborious part. Discard the grey skins and weigh 150g/5oz of the beans for your purée. Any extra can be kept to serve in another dish.

Previous pages: A lucky Oyster Bar customer is about to receive a bowl of fresh prawns.
Opposite: This lobster and broad bean dish perfectly epitomizes the colours of summer.

Place the beans, garlic and olive oil in a blender and mix until completely smooth. For this amount of purée, I find it best to use a hand-held stick blender as you can mix small amounts and you end up with a very smooth finish. At this stage the purée will be a little too thick, so add a couple of 1–2 tablespoons of water and blend again until completely smooth, season and put to one side.

To cook the lobsters, you will need a large saucepan that can hold all your lobsters. Fill with well-salted water and bring to the boil. Now add your lobsters and boil rapidly for 10 minutes. Remove the lobsters from the water and leave to cool for 3–4 minutes until you can touch them.

Cut the lobster in half lengthways with a large chopping knife by holding the lobster flat with one hand and inserting the blade in its back behind its eyes and chopping down towards its tail splitting the bottom half in two. Then turn the lobster around so it faces the other direction and chop the top of the head in half so you end up with two pieces. Discard the dark thread of digestive tract from the tail. Remove the tails from the shells and crack open the claws to remove the meat. If the lobsters have a coral, which will turn red during cooking, it is a very nice touch to remove this and mix it through the vinaigrette before serving. Place all the meat on a dish, brush with olive oil and cover with foil to keep warm in a preheated low oven while finishing the dish.

To serve, warm the purée and then place a couple of spoonfuls on each plate, spreading it out with the back of a spoon. Place 2 halves of lobster tail and 2 claws on each plate, dress with the vinaigrette and serve.

Matthew admiring the beauty of two Dorset lobsters prior to cooking.

Fresh wild salmon, whether it is English or Scottish is a wonderful fish: firm flesh, with a flavour of its own. Wild salmon may cost three or four times the price of farmed salmon, but it is money well spent.

8 tomatoes
125ml/4fl oz extra virgin olive oil
1 bunch of basil, finely chopped
1 garlic clove, finely chopped
3 shallots, finely chopped
grated zest of 1 lemon
4 pieces of wild salmon fillet, about 200g/7oz each
olive oil, for cooking
salt and freshly ground black pepper
4 lemon wedges, to serve

SERVES 4

Fillet of wild salmon with sauce vierge

Place a large pan of water on the stove and bring to the boil. Score a small x on the bottom each tomato, with the point of a sharp knife. Now plunge the tomatoes into the boiling water for 15 seconds. Remove the tomatoes and hold them under the cold tap to cool. You will now find the skins easy to remove with your fingers. When this is done cut the tomatoes into quarters, and, with a small knife make a scooping motion to remove the seeds and innards. You should be left with just the flesh now. Cut this into 5mm/¼ inch dice and place in the olive oil. Add the basil, garlic, shallots and lemon zest, stir and season. Leave to let the flavours marry whilst you grill the fish.

I find it best to use one of those ribbed grill pans. Season and lightly oil the fish. Make sure the pan is hot and cook the fish for 4–5 minutes on each side.

To serve, spoon a generous amount of the sauce on each portion of fish and garnish with a wedge of lemon.

Clockwise from top left: Kitchen staff ready to take on any challenge; a Bibendum menu; Terence enjoying a cigar (pre-smoking ban) with a collection of glassware he had designed for the restaurant; the silver cigar humidor.

This rich creamy cheesecake is of the uncooked variety and is best made when the strawberries are at their ripest and juiciest. It would be preferable to make it a day in advance to allow plenty of time for it to set properly.

200g/7oz strawberries, hulled, plus extra strawberries, for lining
  (approximately 250g/8oz)
1 recipe Sponge Cake, without the Amaretto (see page 219)
500g/1lb mascarpone
150g/5oz icing sugar
3 gelatine leaves
400g/14oz whipping cream, whipped to ribbon stage

STRAWBERRY SAUCE
250g/8oz strawberries, hulled
100g/3½oz icing sugar
juice of ½ lemon
2 tablespoons strawberry eau de vie or Cointreau

SERVES 6–10

Strawberry cheesecake

Purée the strawberries in a blender, or press through a sieve. Put the purée into a saucepan and bring to the boil. Stir so it does not catch on the bottom. Allow some of the liquid to evaporate whilst boiling. The volume of the purée should reduce by half so you are left with 100g/3½oz strong strawberry purée. Pass it through a fine sieve to remove the seeds and then allow it to cool completely.

Fit the sponge in the bottom of a 20-cm/8-inch cake ring that is 6cm/2½ inches high. Line the inside of the ring with strawberries that have been cut in half. Make sure the flat cut edge faces out. When the cheesecake is unmoulded at the end you get a very nice effect on the edge.

Whip the mascarpone, sugar and cold strawberry purée until well mixed. Soak the gelatine in cold water and when soft remove and melt on a gentle heat until liquid. Fold this into the cheese mixture then combine with the cream, using a spatula. Spoon into the ring and level the top with a palette knife. Refrigerate overnight to set.

To make the strawberry sauce, purée everything together in a blender and pass through a fine sieve.

To serve, remove the cake ring from the cheesecake, taking care not to dislodge the strawberries. Serve slices accompanied by some of the sauce.

Waiting at the bar to collect drinks for guests.

Gooseberries often seem to be overlooked these days. We use them a lot at the restaurant when they are in season. This is by far the most popular way we serve them.

250g/8oz gooseberries, topped and tailed
250ml/8fl oz elderflower cordial
750ml/1 ¼ pints double cream
icing sugar, to taste, if necessary

SERVES 6

Gooseberry and elderflower fool

Put the gooseberries in a saucepan with the cordial and bring to the boil. Turn the heat down and let them simmer away for 20–30 minutes or until they have all burst and you are left with a mushy slop. Leave to cool completely and then chill in the fridge.

When it is completely cold all the way through, whisk the cream and the gooseberry mix together until thick. Taste the mixture now and if it is not sweet enough for you add 1–2 tablespoons icing sugar and whisk again. Spoon into glass tumblers and allow to set in the fridge for at least 1 hour. Serve with Madeleines (see page 169).

Clockwise from top left: An original Bibendum chandelier; the reception desk and the reservations book – a vital part of any good restaurant; light from the stained glass window casting patterns on the wall; food being delivered.

The refreshing crunch and tingling on the tongue of a perfectly made granita is a joy on a hot summer's day. If you want to embellish it further, a spoonful of mint flavoured crème chantilly on top is delicious. This dessert is easy enough to make, all you need is a freezer, and of course it can be made several days in advance. The trick to getting the crystals of your granita a good size is to freeze the mixture in a shallow metal tray (a very clean roasting tin will do) and to stir it with a fork every 20 minutes.

I medium-sized watermelon
juice of 1/2 lemon
50g/2oz icing sugar
leaves of 1/2 bunch of mint, finely chopped

MINT CRÈME CHANTILLY *(optional)*
250ml/8fl oz double cream
I teaspoon vanilla essence
2 tablespoons crème de menthe
50g/2oz icing sugar

SERVES 6–8

Watermelon and mint granita

Cut the melon into wedges and scoop out the flesh. Pop it in the food processor or blender and pulse until you have a slush. Place this in a fine sieve and push through to create the juice. Measure 1 litre/1 3/4 pints watermelon juice and add the lemon juice. Whisk in the sugar and then stir in the mint leaves.

Pour the liquid into a shallow metal tray and place in the freezer. Then every 20 minutes or so open the freezer and stir the liquid. As crystals start to form scrape them away from the edge. This process will need to be repeated until you have a tray full of pink crystals, which can take 3–4 hours.

If making the mint crème chantilly, place all the ingredients in a large bowl and whisk until thick. Chill before serving.

Serve the granita in tumblers or other suitable glasses, embellished by a spoonful of the mint crème chantilly.

Watermelon and mint granita – the perfect cooler for a hot day.

White peaches are best if you can get them, however, yellow will make an admirable substitute. At the restaurant we also use apricots – just remember to reduce the cooking time.

200g/7oz amaretti biscuits
75g/3oz unsalted butter
150g/5oz flaked almonds
grated zest of 2 oranges
100g/3½oz ricotta
2 egg yolks
50ml/2fl oz Armagnac
6 peaches
4 tablespoons caster sugar
1 bottle of port
crème fraîche, to serve

SERVES 6

Roast peaches with ricotta, almonds and port

In a large mixing bowl, crush the biscuits with the end of a rolling pin. Then by hand mix in the butter, almonds, orange zest, ricotta, egg yolks and Armagnac to form a cohesive mass. Split the peaches in half and remove the stones. Place the peaches, cut side up in a roasting tin.

Put a walnut-sized piece of the filling on each peach half. Scatter 1 teaspoon of sugar over each half and add the port. Roast the peaches in a preheated oven, 180°C (350°F), Gas Mark 4, for 20 minutes. Remove the peaches from the tin and keep warm. Pour the port into a saucepan. Boil to reduce to a syrup. If the port is not sweet enough add a touch more sugar.

To serve, give 2 peach halves to each person and drizzle with the syrup. Decorate with a spoonful of crème fraîche.

Summer peaches fit for a King.

BY GRAHAM WILLIAMS, FORMER GENERAL MANAGER

Truffle lady: A tricky evening service

During my time as General Manager at Bibendum Restaurant, I spent many happy hours caring for the guests and looking after the well-being of the staff employed at the Restaurant. There have been high points and low points, laughter and, sometimes, tears. I think I must have felt every emotion known to man during my 18 years spent at the helm of one of the capital's great restaurants. There are so many moments I could share with you, but the tale that follows is one of my fondest memories.

One Sunday evening an American lady arrived who seemed a little perplexed by the menu. I went to offer some help to which she replied, 'I don't know what any of this is. Could you please explain what these dishes are?' The menu at Bibendum, as many will know, is pretty extensive offering some 20 first courses and 20 main courses. So I ploughed my way through the menu delighting in making the dishes come to life. Veal sweetbreads with fresh morels in cream sauce, côte de boeuf, sauce béarnaise, fillet of sea bass with sauce vierge to name but a few. I felt extremely pleased with myself and rather hungry after describing every dish. I waited for some hint of an order when she announced, 'What do you have for vegetarians?'

I was completely gob smacked. Trying not to appear too devastated I suggested the Piedmontese peppers – a red pepper stuffed with the ripest tomato and thin slivers of garlic, roasted very slowly in olive oil. I noted that the anchovy fillet topping could be omitted providing a delicious vegetarian first course. The lady was happy with my suggestion and minutes later I saw one of the waiters leaving with the dish. To my horror, my instruction to the kitchen had been ignored and there sitting splendidly on top of the pepper was the salty slither of anchovy fillet. I failed to catch up with the waiter as he proudly presented the pepper. She looked horrified, as did I, and I apologized and quickly removed the plate. I returned to the kitchen, picked off the offending anchovy, swore at the young larder chef and returned the pepper to the table.

'Excuse me' says the lady. 'May I ask did you just remove the anchovy and return the pepper to me?' I blushed and admitted that was exactly what I had done. 'Well I can't eat it. Please get me the menu again.' Oh dear I thought. This could go on forever. I handed over the menu with the evening specials card that I had previously forgotten. She looked at the card and exclaimed, 'Oh! You have black truffles with scrambled egg. Yes that is just what I want.' I then decided it might just be fun to tease Madam slightly. 'Oh dear' I say. 'I don't think you could possibly have that dish.'

'And why on earth not?' she replied.

'Well, I mean the truffles. They've been on the end of a pigs nose.' She shrieked and ordered a green salad. I left the table and returned to kitchen where I shared the tale with Simon who thought the whole thing side-splittingly funny.

The athletic prowess of the waiting staff together with a cheerful demeanour is essential for a successful restaurant.

JERUSALEM ARTICHOKE SOUP WITH CEPES

STROZZAPRETI WITH TOMATO SAUCE AND SAGE

MUSSELS IN GEWÜRZTRAMINER WITH CHIVES AND CREAM

SMOKED COD'S ROE WITH DEVILLED EGG MOUSSE AND PICKLED CUCUMBER

ROAST MALLARD WITH SPICED QUINCE COMPOTE

FILLET OF HAKE WITH ANCHOIADE CRUST, BEURRE BLANC AND CHIVES

ROAST GROUSE WITH BREAD SAUCE

CALVES' SWEETBREADS WITH PARSNIP PUREE AND SAUCE CHARCUTIERE

CREME RENVERSEE AUX RAISINS

BLACKCURRANT POACHED PEARS WITH CHAMPAGNE SYLLABUB AND MADELEINES

CARAMELIZED ORANGE RICE PUDDING

SUSSEX POND PUDDING

Autumn

Recipes by Matthew Harris

Monsieur Bibendum's table setting from one of the restaurant posters.

This thick, creamy and comforting soup is perfect when served with a garnish of fresh sautéed cèpes, garlic and parsley. Of course, you can use other wild mushrooms, but you cannot beat cèpes, can you?

50g/2oz dried cèpes
4 tablespoons vegetable oil
2 large onions, chopped
8 garlic cloves, roughly chopped
1 sprig of thyme
4 bay leaves
1 leek, chopped
2 celery sticks, chopped
1kg/2lb Jerusalem artichokes, peeled
1.5 litres/2½ pints chicken stock (see page 76)
200g/7oz fresh cèpes, thinly sliced
2 garlic cloves, finely chopped
2 teaspoons chopped parsley
100ml/3½fl oz double cream
salt and freshly ground black pepper

SERVES 6–8

Jerusalem artichoke soup with cèpes

Soak the dried cèpes in a cup of warm water, to reconstitute them, for 10 minutes.

In a large saucepan, heat the oil and gently fry the onions until soft.

Then drain the cèpes and squeeze with your hand – keep the brown water to add to the soup later. Add the cèpes to the onions and fry until all is golden. Now add the roughly chopped garlic along with the thyme and bay leaves. Fry for 2 minutes and then add the leek, celery and artichokes. Stir these around in the bottom of the saucepan for 5 minutes. Then add the brown cèpe-flavoured water and the chicken stock. Bring to the boil and then turn down to a simmer. Allow to cook for 30 minutes.

About 10 minutes before the soup is ready, sauté the fresh cèpes in butter until golden. Add the finely chopped garlic along with the parsley. Season with salt and pepper.

Remove the soup from the heat and fish out the thyme and bay leaves puréeing until completely smooth. If the soup is a little too thick, add a bit more chicken stock. Season with salt and pepper and stir in the double cream just before serving. Serve with a spoonful of the fresh cèpe mixture on top of each bowl of soup.

The hubble bubble of the kitchen in preparation for a busy day ahead.

Made with dry stale bread these type of gnocchi are easy to make and less fiddly to roll than potato gnocchi. The name refers to the rope that a monk or priest ties around his waist to hold in his robe. When you roll out the mixture into a long thin sausage shape you can see what is meant, with a bit of imagination.

150g/5oz dry stale bread, torn into 3–5-cm/1 ¼–2-inch chunks
150ml/¼ pint milk
200g/7oz spinach
2 egg yolks
50g/2oz Parmesan, grated, plus extra, to serve
¼ teaspoon nutmeg
2 garlic cloves, finely chopped
plain flour, for rolling
unsalted butter
40 sage leaves
salt and freshly ground black pepper

TOMATO SAUCE
8 ripe tomatoes
50ml/2fl oz extra virgin olive oil
1 large onion, finely chopped
2 garlic cloves, finely chopped
1 tablespoon tomato purée
1 teaspoon chopped sage
¼ teaspoon grated orange zest

SERVES 4

Strozzapretti with tomato sauce and sage

Put the bread and milk in a bowl, mix, and then leave to soak overnight in the fridge. The next day place the bread and milk in a colander in the sink and squeeze out as much of the milk as you can by hand. Tip into a bowl.

To make the tomato sauce, score the tomatoes on the bottoms with a small knife and blanch in boiling water for 30 seconds, remove and run under the tap to cool. Remove the skins with the tip of a knife and your thumb and roughly chop the flesh. In a saucepan, heat the oil and fry the onion gently for 10 minutes or until soft and pale golden. Then add the garlic and tomato purée and fry for a further 5 minutes. Add the sage, orange zest and chopped tomatoes and turn the heat down. Allow to cook gently, uncovered, for 20 minutes whisking occasionally to break up the tomato or until a lot of the juice from the tomatoes has evaporated and you are left with a rich thick tomato sauce. Season with salt and pepper.

While the sauce is cooking, return to the strozzapretti. Bring a large pan of water to the boil, add the spinach and boil briefly. Remove the spinach from the pan and place it in a bowl of iced water. This will stop it cooking and preserve the greenness

If you are hungry on a cold autumn day, this is the dish for you.

of the leaves. Strain off the water and squeeze out the spinach to remove as much of the water as possible. The best way to do this is to bundle it up in a tea towel and squeeze the towel. Roughly chop the spinach then add it to the bowl of squeezed-out bread. Now add the egg yolks, Parmesan, nutmeg, garlic and salt and pepper. You should have a dough-like mass with a consistency similar to bread dough. Roll it out on a floured work surface into long finger-thick rope-like lengths. If the dough is a little too sticky, work in a little flour by hand until the right consistency is achieved. However, it is best if no extra flour is added as the strozzapretti will remain more tender. The trick is to make sure the bread and spinach are very well squeezed in the beginning.

Once you have the rope-like length cut it at 3-cm/1¼-inch intervals to give bite-size lumps. Bring a large saucepan of water to the boil. Add the strozzapretti and cook them for 3 minutes – they will float when cooked. Cook them in batches, if necessary, to avoid them being crowded in the pan. Remove them with a slotted spoon and put in iced water to cool. After 10 minutes remove from the water using the slotted spoon and place on a tray of kitchen paper to drain.

When ready to eat, sauté the strozzapretti in a non-stick frying pan in a little butter until golden all over. Add the sage leaves towards the end of cooking and allow these to crisp up in the butter.

To serve, heat 6–8 tablespoons of tomato sauce and place a couple of spoonfuls in the bottom of warm serving bowls, spoon the strozzapretti on top with some of the sage leaves and a little of the butter. Sprinkle with grated Parmesan and serve.

Preparing strozzapretti.

A refined version of the French classic moules à la crème. The Gewürztraminer's fruity flavour works wonders with the mussels.

2 kg/4 lb mussels
100g/3 ¹/₂oz unsalted butter
50g/2oz diced carrot (2–3mm/about ¹/₈ inch square)
50g/2oz diced leek (2–3mm/about ¹/₈ inch square)
50g/2oz diced celery (2–3mm/about ¹/₈ inch square)
50g/2oz shallot, finely chopped
2 garlic cloves, finely chopped
375ml/13fl oz Gewürztraminer
125ml/4fl oz double cream
¹/₂ lemon
1 bunch of chives, finely chopped
salt and freshly ground black pepper

SERVES 4

Mussels in Gewürztraminer with chives and cream

First make sure the mussels are clean by rinsing them in cold water and going through them one at a time, discarding any open mussels, and removing the beard that is a stringy bit that can stick out the side of the shells; if you just pinch it with your fingers and pull hard, it will come away.

In a large saucepan with a lid, melt the butter and gently fry the vegetables and garlic without colouring them, stirring frequently. After 5 minutes add the wine and boil until it has reduced by half. Now add the mussels and cover the pan with a lid. Gently shake the pan to and fro keeping the lid on with one hand and holding on to the pan handle with the other. After 3 minutes lift the lid and peek at the mussels; if they are not yet all open return to the heat and shake for another minute or two until open. Discard any that remain closed.

Now add the cream and stir it in. Taste the liquid in the bottom of the pan and season with salt and pepper and a squeeze of lemon juice. You are now ready to serve so stir in the chopped chives and serve in deep bowls, making sure to pour in plenty of sauce.

Mussels in Gewürztraminer, a delicious combination and a perfect start to a meal.

Smoked cod's roe takes me back to my childhood in Sussex where we had a smokery up the road and their cod's roe was the best. These days at the restaurant, I buy it from H. Forman & Sons; it has just the right moisture/firmness balance and a good flavour of smoke.

480–600g/15oz–1lb 3oz smoked cods' roe, thinly sliced
lemon wedges, to garnish
salt and freshly ground black pepper

EGG MOUSSE
40g/1 1/2oz unsalted butter
5 eggs
1/4 teaspoon cayenne pepper
1 gelatine leaf
150ml/1/4 pint double cream

PICKLED CUCUMBER
2 cucumbers
100ml/3 1/2fl oz white wine vinegar
2 tablespoons caster sugar

SERVES 6

Smoked cod's roe with devilled egg mousse and pickled cucumber

To make the egg mousse, bring a saucepan of water to the boil. Place a mixing bowl that will fit on top over the pan. Add the butter and allow it to melt. In another bowl, whisk the eggs with the cayenne lightly, just to mix, and season. Now add this to the butter and whisk gently. The eggs will start to scramble but because they are cooking over water you will have more control and they will cook slower. Allow them to cook to the consistency of thick custard. Then remove from the heat and cool over a bowl of iced water, whilst stirring. Soak the gelatine in cold water until floppy and then melt it gently in a saucepan – do not let the gelatine boil or it will not set the mousse. Stir the gelatine into the eggs. Next semi-whip the cream and then fold it into the eggs. When mixed, pour into a serving dish and allow to set in the fridge for at least 3 hours.

To prepare the pickled cucumbers, slice the cucumbers as thinly as you can. Now lightly salt the cucumber and place in a colander. The salt will draw out some of the moisture. Leave for 30 minutes. Meanwhile, in a bowl, stir the vinegar and sugar together until dissolved. After 30 minutes, transfer the cucumber to a clean tea towel, roll it up and squeeze out as much of the remaining juice as you can. Tip the cucumber into the vinegar and season with salt and pepper. Transfer to a serving dish.

To serve, season the roe with pepper and place on a dish garnished with lemon wedges. Let everyone help themselves to the roe, mousse and cucumber and make sure there is plenty of hot buttered toast.

Many guests have a glass of Champagne while they peruse the menu.

The aromatic and sweet compote can be served with many things besides mallard: it works well with pork and is superb mixed through apple crumble. Mallard is a lovely game bird when served pink and juicy so be careful not to overcook it or it will become dry and tough.

QUINCE COMPOTE SYRUP
4 large quinces
1kg/2lb caster sugar
1 litre/1 ¾ pints water
4 bay leaves
12 cloves
1 cinnamon stick
juice and zest of 2 oranges
juice and zest of 2 lemons

MALLARDS
50g/2oz unsalted butter, softened
2 mallards
125ml/4fl oz red wine
100ml/3 ½ fl oz strong jellied chicken (see page 76) or game stock
salt and freshly ground black pepper

SERVES 4

Roast mallard with spiced quince compote

To make the quince compote syrup, peel the quinces, cut them into quarters then remove the core. Put the quarters of quince in the fridge. Place the peelings and core in a saucepan with all the other compote ingredients and bring to the boil. Once boiling, reduce the heat to a very gentle simmer and leave for 3 hours. The syrup will develop a lovely deep rust colour. After 3 hours sieve out all the bits from the syrup then return it to the saucepan. Now add the quince quarters and simmer gently for 1 hour or until soft. Leave to cool before refrigerating until needed.

Smear the butter all over the birds and season with salt and pepper. Heat a large flamproof dish on the hob and fry the birds, breast-side down until the breasts are golden. Then place in a preheated oven, 200°C (400°F), Gas Mark 6, and cook for 15–20 minutes so they remain pink. Remove from the oven, transfer the birds to another dish and allow to rest somewhere warm. Return the roasting dish to the

Roast game birds are one of Bibendum's autumn specialities.

hob to make a quick gravy. Add the red wine and bring to the boil. Using a whisk, scrape away the bits stuck to the bottom of the dish and allow the wine to reduce by half. Add the stock and 50ml/2fl oz of the quince compote syrup and allow this to reduce some more until a tasty, slightly sweet gravy is achieved.

Now warm up 4 quince quarters and some of the syrup. Carve the mallards, and pour any of the blood and roasting juices into the gravy. The leftover quince quarters can be saved to be serve with cold meats or terrines – they will last for ages in the refrigerator.

Serve half a bird each with a quarter of a quince and spoon over the gravy.

Opposite: The roast mallard has been sliced for the customer's convenience.
Above: Monsieur Bibendum is etched into the glass of the waiter's station. He keeps an eye on everything.

Anchovies! I love them. The Spanish ones are the best; Cantabrian canned in olive oil. They are delicious with crusty toasted sourdough and butter. But here they are served with another fish highly prized in Spain, hake. Incidentally, if you have anchoïade left over, it will keep in the fridge for a week and is great on toast for breakfast, homemade Gentleman's Relish.

4 hake fillets, about 200g/7oz each
4 tablespoons dried breadcrumbs
salt and freshly ground black pepper

ANCHOÏADE
100g/3¹/₂oz best-quality salted anchovies in oil, drained
2 egg yolks
100ml/3¹/₂ fl oz olive oil
1 garlic clove, chopped
leaves from a sprig of thyme

BEURRE BLANC
2 shallots, chopped
50ml/2fl oz white wine vinegar
125g/4oz unsalted butter, cut into small knobs
2 teaspoons chopped chives

SERVES 4

Fillet of hake with anchoïade crust, beurre blanc and chives

The anchoïade is best made with one of those hand-held stick blenders. Put everything into a bowl and blend them together. They will mix into a smooth brown paste. Season generously with black pepper, then set aside.

To make the beurre blanc, place the shallots in a saucepan with the vinegar and boil until the vinegar has all evaporated. Remove from the heat and start whisking in the butter a knob at a time. The residual heat in the pan will melt the butter and so long as you keep whisking, the sauce will emulsify. Season with salt and pepper and leave on the back of the stove to keep warm.

Put a teaspoon of anchoïade on top of each piece of fish and spread out evenly with a palette knife. Place the fish on a non-stick baking sheet and cover the anchoïade with a generous coating of the breadcrumbs. Bake in a preheated oven, 220°C (425°F), Gas Mark 7, for about 12 minutes, during which time the breadcrumbs will toast to create a crust. The hake should just flake when tested with the point of a sharp knife. To serve, place a portion of fish on each plate. Stir the chives into the sauce and spoon some around each piece of hake.

Careful and professional preparation of the quality ingredients is a vital part of the chef's job.

The glorious twelfth – not so glorious for the grouse. The opening day of the grouse season is certainly not the best day to eat birds shot that day; they are really at their best about a week later, after they have been hung and their flavour matured. If you buy oven-ready grouse ask the butcher to leave in the heart and liver as they will be used to enhance the flavour of the sauce, and make a tasty liver croûte to serve the bird on.

125g/4oz unsalted butter, softened, at room temperature
4 grouse
50ml/2fl oz brandy
1 garlic clove, chopped
1 teaspoon redcurrant jelly
250ml/8fl oz strong jellied chicken stock (see page 76)
4 slices of white bread, crust removed
salt and freshly ground black pepper
watercress, to garnish (optional)

BREAD SAUCE
400ml/14fl oz milk
1 teaspoon whole cloves
1 onion, chopped
1 sprig of thyme
3 bay leaves
100g/3½oz fresh breadcrumbs

SERVES 4

Roast grouse with bread sauce

To make the bread sauce, bring the milk with everything in it except the breadcrumbs, to the boil and then remove from the heat and leave to infuse, covered, for at least 3 hours. Boil again and pass through a fine sieve. Stir in the breadcrumbs and keep warm on the back of the stove.

Smear the butter generously all over the birds and season well. Roast in a preheated oven, 220°C (425°F), Gas Mark 7, for 20–30 minutes; 20 minutes will leave the flesh pink on the bone, moist and juicy, 30 minutes will cook it through.

Checking the ingredients as they are delivered to see that they meet the required standards.

When cooked remove from the oven and, with a spoon, scrape the heart and liver out of the cavities of the grouse into the roasting tin. Place the birds in another dish and keep warm.

Season the livers and hearts and fry on the hob in the roasting tin. After a couple of minutes, remove the tin from the heat, stand back a bit and pour in the brandy; it will ignite. Allow the alcohol to evaporate for 2 minutes before returning the tin to the heat. Then add the garlic and redcurrant jelly. With a whisk scrape away at the bottom of the tin to remove any tasty stuck-on bits. Add the chicken stock, boil and reduce to a tasty gravy. Pass through a fine sieve and keep the gravy warm.

Now empty the contents of the sieve onto a chopping board and chop vigorously to a smoothish paste.

Toast the bread and spread a layer of the paste on each piece to make liver croûte.

To serve, place a liver croûte on each plate with a grouse on top, pour over some gravy, and if you like, garnish with a bunch of watercress. Serve the bread sauce on the side.

A busy scene in the Café in the Michelin Building entrance lobby – this was originally used as the tyre fitting bay.

Offal in its various forms has long been a favourite of mine both to cook and eat. Sweetbreads are up there at the top of the list along with brains. Calves' sweetbreads will have to be ordered in advance from your butcher as very few butchers these days would risk buying them in without a particular request.

1kg/2lb calves' sweetbreads
vegetable oil
salt and freshly ground black pepper

PARSNIP PUREE
750g/1 1/2lb parsnips, cut into chunks
1.2 litres/2 pints milk
4 garlic cloves
1 sprig of thyme
75g/3oz unsalted butter

SAUCE CHARCUTIERE
50g/2oz unsalted butter
1 shallot, finely chopped
1/2 teaspoon mustard powder
1/2 teaspoon redcurrant jelly
250ml/8fl oz white wine
125ml/4fl oz strong veal or chicken stock (see page 76)
25g/1oz cornichons, thinly sliced
1 tablespoon Dijon mustard

SERVES 4

Calves' sweetbreads with parsnip purée and sauce charcutière

To prepare the sweetbreads, bring a large pan of salted water to the boil. Drop the sweetbreads in and allow to simmer for 6 minutes. Take off the heat, remove them from the pan and leave to cool in the refrigerator until they are cool enough for you to be able to handle them. Now peel off the outer membrane with your fingers; be sure to get it all off as it is rubbery and unpleasant to eat. Divide the sweetbreads into 4 equal portions and season with salt and pepper.

To make the parsnip purée, place the parsnips in a saucepan with the milk, garlic and thyme. Bring to the boil and reduce to a simmer until cooked, about 12 minutes. Check they are cooked with the point of a knife. Remove the parsnips, garlic and thyme from the milk and place in a blender. Discard the milk. Add the butter to the parsnips and blend until smooth. Season with salt and pepper then pass through a fine sieve. Warm through.

Sweetbreads, crisp on the outside, creamy inside – delicious. Bibendum specializes in offal, often a rarity these days.

Meanwhile, make the sauce: melt 25g/1oz of the butter in a saucepan and sweat the shallot until soft and golden brown. Add the mustard powder, redcurrant jelly and white wine. Simmer until the liquid is reduced by two-thirds. Add the stock and bring back to the boil, add the cornichons and whisk in the Dijon mustard. Now add the remaining butter, whisking constantly. Season and set aside, but keep warm.

Heat a little oil in a large frying pan and sauté the sweetbreads (in batches, if your pan isn't big enough) for 5 minutes each side or until golden brown and crusty on both sides. You can tell when they are cooked because they have a firmness to the touch like a medium rare steak.

To serve, spoon a portion of the parsnip purée on each plate and put the sweetbreads on top, then spoon the sauce around the edge like a moat.

Few people realize what a huge amount of preparation goes on in the kitchen before a lunch or dinner service – it's an 8am start and an afternoon of intense work.

This is a great version of crème caramel but you must remember to soak the raisins in Armagnac for a couple of days before using them so they become really potent.

6 tablespoons raisins soaked in enough Armagnac to cover
for at least 2 days
450ml/³⁄₄ pint milk
I vanilla pod
5 eggs
50g/2oz caster sugar

CARAMEL
200g/7oz caster sugar
100ml/3 ¹⁄₂fl oz water

SERVES 6

Crème renversée aux raisins

You will need 6 ramekins or similar that will hold 125ml/4fl oz. Spread these out ready to pour the caramel into. Next, place the sugar and water into a saucepan and bring to the boil. Continue to boil until the water is evaporated and the sugar starts to turn to caramel. Stir with a wooden spoon so the caramel colours evenly. When the caramel is dark brown (but not black) remove from the heat and quickly pour about I tablespoonful of caramel into the bottom of each ramekin. It should spread out and give an even covering on the bottom about 3mm/ ¹⁄₈ inch thick. While it is still warm remove the raisins from the Armagnac and sprinkle about I tablespoonful onto the caramel in each ramekin. Now place the ramekins in an ovenproof dish with a little space between each one and put to one side until later.

Pour the milk into a saucepan. Split the vanilla pod and using a knife scrape the seeds out into the milk. Add the split pod, bring to the boil, whisk and remove from the heat.

Crack the eggs into a bowl, add the sugar and whisk to mix. Now stir in the hot milk and whisk. Pass this mixture through a fine sieve. Carefully pour the mixture into the ramekins to fill them. Pour hot water into the oven dish until it is half-way up the ramekins. Place in a preheated oven, 140°C (275°F), Gas Mark 1, and cook for 40–50 minutes or until set. You can tell when they are set by inserting a small knife into the custard and pulling it out. When it comes out clean, the custard is cooked. Then allow to cool before refrigerating. These are best when left to set overnight.

To serve, gently warm the bottom of each ramekin in a bowl of hot water for 10–20 seconds then run a knife around the inside edge to loosen the custard, and turn the dish upside down onto a plate. Then caramel will run out around the edge to make a little sauce.

Clockwise from top left: A sommelier in the restaurant; the Oyster Bar wine list; Simon preparing a prawn cocktail in the Café; ice for the fish counter.

This dessert is a wonderful melange of flavours. The pears are poached in a wine and blackcurrant syrup and then served with creamy syllabub and warm Madeleines. This is a decadent and delicious delight.

PEARS
1 bottle white wine
1 cinnamon stick
1 vanilla pod, split
6 bay leaves
grated zest of 1 lemon
grated zest of 1 orange
1kg/2lb caster sugar
500g/1lb frozen blackcurrants
100ml/3½fl oz crème de cassis
8 pears

MADELEINES
3 eggs
150g/5oz caster sugar
50g/2oz honey
125g/4oz unsalted butter
125g/4oz flour
1½ teaspoons baking powder

SYLLABUB
350ml/12fl oz double cream
150ml/¼ pint Champagne
2 tablespoons Cognac
75g/3oz icing sugar

SERVES 8

Blackcurrant poached pears with Champagne syllabub and Madeleines

Place everything for the pears in a saucepan, except the pears, and bring to the boil. Reduce the heat and allow to simmer for 20 minutes. Meanwhile, peel the pears. When the poaching syrup is ready place the pears in it standing up, with a saucer on top to keep them submerged, and gently poach for 30 minutes. Do not let them boil rapidly, let them just tick over. Remove from the heat and allow them to cool completely in the syrup, then refrigerate in the syrup.

To make the Madeleines, whisk the eggs, sugar and honey together in a food mixer for 5–8 minutes until airy and firm. Meanwhile, melt the butter in a saucepan and allow it to brown. Add the flour and stir with a wooden spoon – this is called a

A firm favourite: the infusion of a pear with wine and blackcurrants is delicious. So are the Madeleines.

roux. Keep stirring and cooking the roux for 4 minutes over the stove. Then remove from the heat and add the roux to the egg mixture, keeping the machine running. When mixed together, whisk in the baking powder. Allow the mixture to rest for 1 hour before cooking. It will keep overnight in the fridge, if you like.

To bake, place 1–2 heaped teaspoons of mixture in non-stick Madeleine moulds and bake in a preheated oven, 180°C (350°F), Gas Mark 4, for 7 minutes. They should be peaked in the middle when cooked. Cook in batches if necessary. Serve warm.

To make the syllabub, whisk all the ingredients together until thick but slightly runny like a sabayon.

To serve the dessert, strain a few blackcurrants from the poaching syrup to put on the plate along with a pear each and some of the syllabub. Serve with at least 2 Madeleines each.

Pears poaching so they become deliciously infused with the syrup flavours.

A comforting nursery pudding with a more adult flavour.

60g/2½oz unsalted butter
100g/3½oz pudding rice
75g/3oz caster sugar
750ml/1¼ pints milk
125ml/4fl oz double cream
rind from 2 oranges
pinch of salt
1 vanilla pod

SERVES 4

Caramelized orange rice pudding

In a flameproof casserole or a saucepan, melt the butter and when liquid add the rice and sugar. Fry this mixture gently for 5–10 minutes until the sugar has caramelized and the grains of rice are nut brown. Now add the milk and cream, orange zest and salt. Split the vanilla pod and use the tip of a knife to scrape the seeds into the pan. Add the pod. Bring the whole to the boil and stir, making sure the rice and sugar mixture, which will have solidified on adding the milk, is dissolved and dispersed.

Cook, uncovered, in a preheated oven, 140°C (275°F), Gas Mark 1, for 2½–3 hours or until just starting to set. Remove from the oven and allow to sit somewhere warm for at least 20 minutes before serving.

The Café in preparation for the morning breakfast rush. Below, a huge selection of French and British cheese is offered at Bibendum.

A very satisfying suet pudding that contains chunks of lemon slowly cooked in sugar and butter combining to make a bitter-sweet filling best served with a dollop of Jersey cream. The name refers to the liquid that leaks from the puddings when served.

PASTRY
400g/13oz self-raising flour
200g/7oz suet
pinch of salt
125ml/4fl oz milk
125ml/4fl oz water

FILLING
2 lemons
unsalted butter (see method)
demerara sugar (see method)

SERVES 4

Sussex pond pudding

Butter 4 x 250ml/8fl oz heatproof plastic pudding basins.

To make the pastry, mix the flour, suet and salt together in a large bowl. Then mixing with your fingers, add the milk and start to work into a dough. When you have added all the milk start to add the water. You may not need all of this. Keep working until you have a dough you can roll out with a rolling pin. Roll the dough out to 3–4mm/1/8–1/4 inch thick and then cut out 4 circles big enough to line the basins. A side plate is a good size to use as a template. Now cut out one-quarter of each circle. Place the remaining three-quarters in each basin, bringing the 2 cut edges together to overlap a little bit. Push the pastry down into the basins, taking care to seal the overlap by pressing firmly. Keep the remaining quarters to use as the lids.

To make the filling, weigh the lemons and then weigh out the same amount of butter and of sugar. Cut the lemons into 1-cm/1/2-inch square chunks – it does not matter if they are not uniform. Do the same with the butter. Mix in a bowl with the sugar and then fill each of the lined basins with the filling.

Now roll the remaining pastry quarters into circles and cut to fit as lids. Pinch the lining and lid firmly together to make a tight seal. Cover the top of each pudding with foil with a pleat folded across it. Place the puddings in a steamer with a tightly fitting lid, over a saucepan of simmering water. Leave to boil gently for 3 hours. Keep an eye on the level of the water level and top up with boiling water, if necessary.

To serve, remove the foil and turn the puddings out into bowls – don't forget the cream!

The finished Sussex pond pudding makes you hungry just looking at it. Overleaf, the pudding in preparation.

SEAN SUTCLIFFE, MANAGING DIRECTOR OF BENCHMARK

Setting the style

I most vividly remember a day-long meeting in the dining room at Barton Court in Terence's home. It was a day that brimmed with sunshine, creative thought, tape measures, bits of wood and fabric, food and an all-consuming enthusiasm. Terence Conran had his sleeves rolled up and three eager young men toiled alongside him with a passion to thrash out the details of the big new project – Bibendum. It was my first experience of creating a restaurant, Simon Hopkinson's (chef) and Joel Kissen's (restaurant manager) second and Terence's third. We measured everything

from cutlery and trays to shoulders and bottoms, leaving no stone unturned in our pursuit of getting it right. It was 21 years ago at the very early days of what has become Benchmark, and it was the first of some 200 plus restaurants that we have been involved in furnishing. I did not know anything about how a restaurant worked, and I had to learn a whole new vocabulary that is a strange mix of French and kitchen slang. I did not know how high tables should be, how a waiters' station worked, and I certainly did not realise how much use and abuse restaurant furniture had to take.

Terence designed furniture that, in keeping with the building, was without compromise. Our task in the workshop was to make the sketches a reality.

The furniture is, in Bibendum fashion, curvaceous, and so we had to make moulds and laminating jigs to create the curved panels. These same moulds still sit at the back of the workshop awaiting a remake that has yet to happen

The building, and its iconic Monsieur Bibendum, led us all on a journey of learning about the joys, or supposed joys, of early motoring – the fun and the freedom and the luxury of it all. And we sought to reflect all of this in the furniture and the fittings of the restaurant and bar. We used all the metaphors we could from the motorcar: perforated leather from Connolly's, chequered flag marquetry and lots of shiny polished metal. We returned endlessly to the Monsieur Bibendum fatness, with the stacked tyre motif making obvious appearances on the wine stands, chairs and finials, and less obvious ones in the table legs that nobody was ever going to see unless they were on the floor drunk. But we had to have a detail so we made it a Bibendum detail.

Everyone in the workshop worked on the restaurant. Sometimes late at night and at weekends Terence would join us to lend a hand with sanding, or just to clear

Every detail of the Restaurant and Oyster Bar was designed with Monsieur Bibendum's shape in mind, from the flower vases to the box trees in the window boxes, clipped like topiary to echo his shape.

up and make tea so we could continue with the making. We were all driven to get this job done to a relentlessly high standard. That was our summer of 1987, and as the opening drew closer we polished walnut, silver plated metalwork and remade anything that we felt was blemished.

As I look at Bibendum 21 years later, with all its original furniture still intact and still looking elegant, I feel just as proud as I did on that day.

BIBENDUM – THE DESIGN BY TERENCE CONRAN

Designing the Bibendum restaurant was one of the most enjoyable jobs of my restaurant designing career (over seventy restaurants to date) firstly because it is such a wonderful building and secondly because the Bibendum and Michelin archive

provides so many charming and inspirational ideas. The shape and details of the chairs, table legs, wine buckets, china and glass and other ceramics bear reference to Mr Bibendum's chubby shape and personality.

Also Simon Hopkinson and Joel Kissin were in place and consultations and discussions about how the restaurant and bar would work in practice were invaluable, something that is rarely possible in the design of new restaurants. Better still Sean and his woodworking team were up and running and keen to make and help detail and prototype a wonderful collection of products for the restaurant.

I was helped by Wendy Wood from Conran and Partners, who took on my sketches and provided the detailed planning of the staircases, lighting, the lift, air conditioning and helped with the coordination of the ceilings, floors and sub-divisions of the spaces and negotiation with the building contractors.

It all has lasted for 21 years with only minor refurbishments; it has gained a rather pleasant patina of hard usage over the years, helped by rigorous cleaning and careful upkeep by the staff.

The final decorative pieces such as the stained glass windows and the etched window glass maps taken from the early Michelin guides and the Michelin cartoons of people connected to the emerging French motor industry made a charming and relevant difference to the ambiance.

The restaurant graphics took inspiration from mosaics in the floors of the building. I always remember Edouard Michelin, great grandson of the original Michelin brothers Edouard and André, visiting the restaurant with his wife and daughter for Saturday lunch a few years ago. He told me how excited he was to see his family heirloom so well appreciated by a young crowd. It was one of my proudest moments to have successfully helped to continue the amazing work of his ancestors.

Terence designed furniture that, in keeping with the building, was without compromise. Walnut wood was chosen for its luxuriance, its sense of the classic and importantly, because it is the colour of a Havana cigar!

E GORDON-BENNETT
1901

GIRARDOT sur
PANHARD

DUCK TERRINE
CURED HERRINGS IN BEETROOT AND HORSERADISH WITH POTATO SALAD
SOUPE DE POISSON
CRAB AND SAFFRON TART

SMOKED HADDOCK FISHCAKES WITH SAUCE MESSINE
ROAST PHEASANT WITH GLAZED APPLES, CHESTNUTS AND CALVADOS SAUCE
LOIN OF VENISON WITH JUNIPER ONION COMPOTE AND POMMES ANNA
SLOW-COOKED PORK BELLY WITH CHORIZO AND SHERRY

ORANGE PANNA COTTA WITH RHUBARB COMPOTE
BAKED APPLE WITH CARAMEL SAUCE AND VANILLA ICE CREAM
TARTE VAUDOISE A LA CREME
MARBLED CHOCOLATE MOUSSE CAKE WITH AMARETTO CREME ANGLAISE

Winter

Recipes by Matthew Harris

Gordon Bennett circa 1901. Fantastic publicity for Michelin.

If you can manage to make this terrine a few days before you plan to serve it the flavours will develop and mature, giving you a much better finished product. As a lot of chopping by hand is involved, a large sharp knife is the order of the day to make things go smoothly.

2 large English ducks
250g/8oz lean veal, finely chopped
125g/4oz pork belly, skin discarded, finely chopped
125g/4oz lardo (salted back fat), skin discarded, finely chopped
100g/3½oz duck livers, finely chopped
2 tablespoons green peppercorns
2 eggs, beaten
1 tablespoon chopped thyme
1 tablespoon chopped parsley
juice and grated zest of 2 oranges
3 tablespoons Madeira
3 tablespoons Cognac
3 tablespoons port
20 thin rashers of rindless streaky bacon
salt and freshly ground black pepper

SERVES 8–12

Duck terrine

Remove the breasts and legs from the duck carcass and pull off the skin. Cut all the meat off the leg bones and finely chop the breast and leg meat. Place all the duck meat with the veal, pork belly, lardo and duck livers in a large bowl and add the green peppercorns, eggs, herbs, orange juice and zest. Mix well.

Pour the Madeira, Cognac and port into a saucepan and warm up. Standing back, light the alcohol with a lighted taper. Remove the pan from the heat and allow the flames to burn themselves out. Once the alcohols are cool, stir into the terrine mix. Season with salt and pepper. Now, heat a frying pan, make a small pattie of the mix and fry it in a little oil until cooked. Allow this to cool and then taste it to check the seasoning. If necessary, add more salt and pepper to the meat mixture.

Now line the terrine, a 1.5kg/3lb terrine mould will suffice. Place the bacon in the bottom with each slice slightly overlapping and the ends hanging over the edge. Then fill the terrine with the mixture and fold the overhanging bacon over the top to cover it. Place the lid on the terrine, or cover it with foil. Stand the terrine in a roasting tin and pour in hot water to come two-thirds of the way up the terrine. Cook in a preheated oven, 150°C (300°F), Gas Mark 2, for 1 hour. Then using a meat probe, check the temperature, it should reach 70°C/120°F. If you don't have a probe, insert a skewer into the centre of the terrine, leave it for 30 seconds then

Clockwise from top left: Preparing sandwiches in the Café; timesheets clocking staff in and out; bill checking; freshly baked bagettes.

withdraw it; if it feels warm, the terrine is done. This might take up to 1 1/2 hours depending on the oven. So it is a good idea to check it every 10 minutes after 1 hour of cooking. When ready remove it from the oven and water bath and leave to stand for 30 minutes.

Meanwhile, cut out a piece of cardboard that will fit just inside the terrine. You can use the base of the terrine as a template. Wrap the cardboard heavily in clingfilm. Remove the lid and place the cardboard on top of the terrine. On top of this place a heavy weight, a brick is ideal, and put everything on a tray to catch any juices that overflow. Leave to cool then put the terrine (with the weights still on it) in the fridge to press overnight.

The next day, remove the weight and put the lid back on the terrine and then leave the terrine at the back of the fridge out of the way of temptation for at least 2 days before serving.

One of the stained glass windows, which casts a blue beam of light across the restaurant on a sunny lunch time. Good, courteous service makes the difference between your enjoyment of a meal and disappointment.

This recipe preserves fresh herring fillets in a pickling liquid so they can be kept in a refrigerator for up to a week (they need at least 48 hours, so plan ahead). Several hours before serving, the fillets are put into a beetroot marinade, where they take on more flavours and are transformed into a starter that is both stunning to the eyes and taste buds.

8–12 herring fillets
500g/1lb small waxy potatoes
1 red onion, thinly sliced
bunch of chives, chopped
salt and freshly ground black pepper

PICKLING LIQUID
1 tablespoon allspice berries
200ml/7fl oz distilled malt vinegar
250g/8oz caster sugar
3 bay leaves
150g/5oz onion, thinly sliced

BEETROOT AND HORSERADISH MARINADE
200g/7oz cold cooked beetroot (not in vinegar)
50g/2oz freshly grated horseradish
150ml/¼ pint plain yoghurt
2 teaspoons caster sugar
150ml/¼ pint crème fraîche

SERVES 4

Cured herrings in beetroot and horseradish with potato salad

To make the pickling liquid, take the allspice berries and place them on a hard surface and crack them by banging with the bottom of a saucepan so they crack into several pieces (not a powder as this will cling to the fish fillets when added). Now put all the pickling liquid ingredients into a saucepan, add 375ml/13fl oz water and bring to the boil. Remove from the heat, allow to cool, then put in the refrigerator for 5 hours until chilled to about 5°C (41°F). Now place the herring fillets in a dish they just fit and then pour over the liquid, making sure the fillets are completely covered. Cover the dish, return to the refrigerator and leave to cure for at least 48 hours.

To make the beetroot and horseradish marinade, put all the ingredients except the crème fraîche into a blender, season, and mix together. When completely smooth, stir in the crème fraîche by hand. The result will be a vibrant pink sloppy purée.

Remove the herrings from the pickling liquid and pat dry with kitchen paper.

A delicious fishy start to a meal – almost a meal in itself.

Cover them with the beetroot marinade and return to the refrigerator for at least 6 hours before serving.

Boil the potatoes in their skins until just tender but cooked through. Drain and rinse under cold running water until cool enough to handle. Peel, and slice thickly.

To serve, place a few potato slices on each plate and then add a few thin slices of raw red onion and season with salt and pepper. Remove the herring fillets from the marinade, scraping off some but not all of the marinade with your fingers. Place 2 or 3 fillets on top of each pile of potatoes and sprinkle with a few chopped chives before serving.

A lot of work goes into making the cured herring starter. The beetroot and horseradish marinade produces this wonderful magenta colour.

This recipe does have a lot of ingredients and certainly involves some effort. However, the result of your hard labour will be stunning. A pungent, intensely flavoured soup that will definitely impress. The traditional garnish of rouille, Gruyère and croutons is an absolute necessity. When buying the fish for the soup tell the fishmonger what you are making and get him to pick out a selection of fish.

lots of olive oil, for frying
3–4kg/6-8lb mixed whole fish to include a selection from the following;
    red mullet, gurnard, conger eel (a piece only), weaver, john dory,
    plaice, sole, rascasse, bass, cut into 5cm/2 inch long chunks
2 large leeks, cut into 3–4-cm/1 1/4–1 1/2-inch chunks
1 head celery, cut into 3–4-cm/1 1/4–1 1/2-inch chunks
5 of each, large onions and large carrots, cut into 3–4-cm/1 1/4–1 1/2-inch chunks
200g/7oz tomato purée
1 bottle each of white wine and red wine
500ml/17fl oz passata
2 garlic bulbs, chopped
1 bunch of thyme
10 of each bay leaves and star anise
2 tablespoons fennel seeds
1 chilli
zest of 1 orange
100ml/3 1/2 fl oz Pernod
1 teaspoon saffron strands
salt and pepper

ROUILLE
4 hard-boiled egg yolks
4 anchovy fillets in oil
2 garlic cloves
2 tablespoons tomato purée
6 egg yolks
2 tablespoons Dijon mustard
1 teaspoon saffron strands
500ml/17fl oz olive oil

CROUTONS
500g/1lb Gruyère, grated
1 large baguette or ficelle, cut into 5mm/1/4 inch slices

SERVES 10–12

Soupe de poisson

You will need a very large saucepan that can hold 15–20 litres/3 1/4–4 1/4 gallons, and a very large frying pan. Heat the frying pan and add a good slug of olive oil. Add some of the fish, but do not overcrowd the pan or the fish will just boil rather than fry. Season with salt and pepper and fry until golden and crusty on both sides.

The Bibendum soupe de poisson is as good if not better, than anything you will get on the south coast of France. It takes a lot of preparation and a lot of ingredients.

Scrape the fish into the saucepan. Repeat until all the fish is done. Now fry the vegetables in batches until golden. Towards the end of frying each batch add some of the tomato purée and let that fry, too. Add to the fish. When you have fried the last batch, deglaze the frying pan with some of the wine and scrape off all the bits off that are stuck to the pan. Add the remaining ingredients, except the saffron, to the saucepan and top it up with water to come about 6–8cm/2¼–3¼ inches above the level of the ingredients. Bring to the boil. Reduce the heat and simmer for 2 hours. The soup will throw up an oily scum to the surface, which needs to be removed regularly by gently immersing a ladle in the top and allowing the scum to spill into it. Pass the soup through a conical sieve or a colander, not a fine strainer. Return it to the saucepan and return to the boil. Now add the saffron. Taste the soup, at this stage it may well be a bit too weak, so allow it to boil away and reduce, tasting it regularly until it is strong in flavour. If necessary adjust the seasoning with a bit more salt.

Meanwhile, make the rouille: place all the ingredients except the oil, in a food processor and blend until smooth. Then, in a thin stream, add the oil as if making mayonnaise. Season with salt and pepper and refrigerate until ready to serve.

To make the croutons, lay the slices of bread on a baking tray and cook in a preheated oven, 150°C (300°F), Gas Mark 2, for 10 minutes or until golden.

Serve the soup in warm deep bowls. Place bowls of rouille, Gruyère and croutons on the table so everyone can help themselves.

Our stalwart fish supplier delivers the finest quality fish and shellfish. Langoustines, lobsters and crab are always delivered live for utmost freshness.

This tart makes a great warm starter. It is really a deluxe quiche, but with its fine pastry and creamy savoury filling it is in a class above anything that you might have had before.

PASTRY
400g/14oz plain flour
250g/8oz cold unsalted butter, cut into small pieces
2 eggs
salt

FILLING
½ recipe Tomato Sauce (see page 145)
75g/3oz brown crab meat (optional)
1 teaspoon saffron threads
900ml/1½ pints double cream
2 garlic cloves, finely chopped
12 egg yolks
300g/10oz white crab meat
2 tablespoons chopped basil
salt and freshly ground black pepper

SERVES 8–12

Crab and saffron tart

To make the pastry, rub the flour and butter together in a large mixing bowl. Alternatively put the flour and butter in a food processor and using the pulse button chop the flour through the butter until you can no longer see it. Then tip this into a bowl and add the eggs and a pinch of salt and work into a dough with your hands. If it is a little dry add a drop of water. When the pastry is made, rest it in the fridge for at least 1 hour before rolling it out and lining a 28-cm/11-inch tart ring with a removable base that is 3cm/1¼ inches deep. Try to roll the pastry as thin as you dare without it cracking. When lined, rest the tart case again in the fridge for 30 minutes before baking blind (see page 98) lined with baking beans in a preheated oven, 180°C (350°F), Gas Mark 4 for 15 minutes. Remove the beans and bake for a further 10 minutes or until golden all over. Put this to one side until the filling is made.

To make the filling, take 5 tablespoons of the tomato sauce and mix it with the brown crab meat, if using, and smear all over the bottom of the tart. Next, place the saffron and 3 tablespoons water in a small pan and bring to the boil. Remove from the heat and leave to infuse for 10 minutes. Put the cream along with the garlic in a saucepan and bring to the boil. Remove from the heat and add the saffron together with its liquid. Place the yolks in a bowl, pour over the cream and mix well. Now add the white crabmeat and basil. Taste the mixture and season with salt and pepper. Ladle into the tart case, filling it up, and bake in a preheated oven, 150°C (300°F), Gas Mark 2, for 30–40 minutes or until set. Remove from the oven and allow to stand for 20 minutes somewhere warm before serving.

A wonderful large fresh crab being cooked.

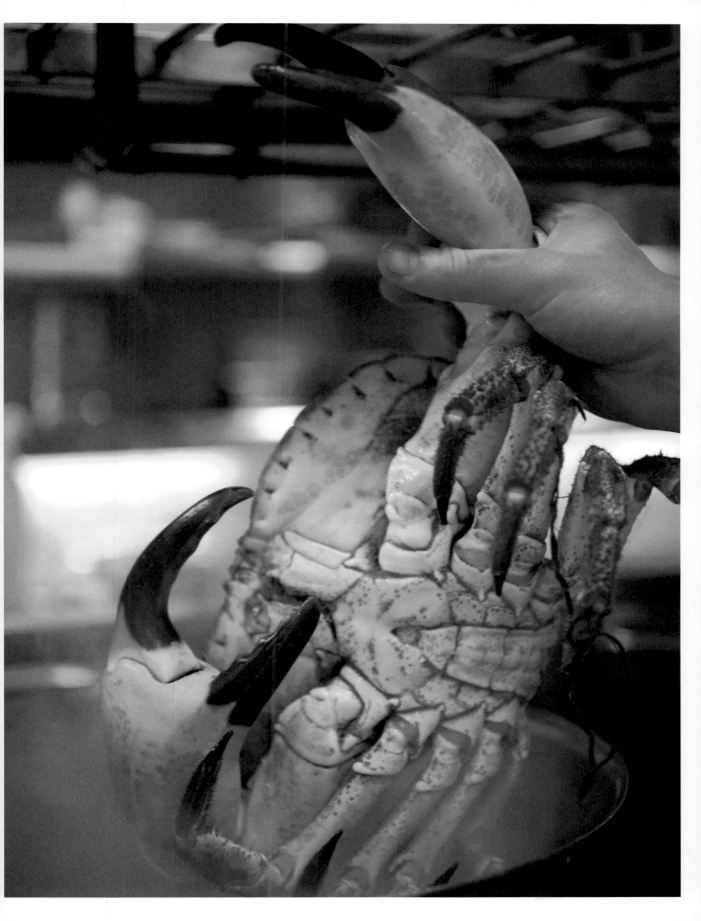

Whenever fishcakes appear on the lunch menu, they are always the most popular dish. Served with this delicious sauce taken from Elizabeth David's *French Provincial Cooking*, it is easy to see why.

500ml/17fl oz milk
600g/1lb 3oz smoked haddock
600g/1lb 3oz mashed potato
3 egg yolks
8 spring onions, finely chopped
2 tablespoons chopped parsley
plain flour, for coating
unsalted butter, for cooking
salt and pepper

SAUCE MESSINE
2 shallots, finely chopped
50g/2oz unsalted butter
250ml/8fl oz double cream
2 teaspoons Dijon mustard
3 egg yolks
1 tablespoon chopped tarragon
1 tablespoon chopped parsley
squeeze of lemon juice

SERVES 4

Smoked haddock fishcakes with sauce messine

Heat the milk in a saucepan and then poach the haddock in it for about 8–12 minutes depending on thickness. Strain off and discard the milk. Remove any skin or bones from the haddock and place the flesh in a large bowl. Add the mashed potato, egg yolks, spring onions and parsley. Mix everything together. Season with salt and pepper. Divide the mixture into 8 and shape them into 2cm/3/4 inch high discs. Refrigerate for 2 hours, to firm up.

To make the sauce messine, fry the shallots in the butter in a saucepan until soft, without colouring. Then pour the cream into a bowl and mix with the mustard. Now pour the cream over the yolks and mix well. Pour the cream mix into the saucepan and cook over a low heat, stirring the whole time until the sauce is thickened to custard-like consistency; do not allow it to boil. Remove from the heat, stir in the herbs and season with the lemon juice and salt and pepper.

To cook the fish cakes, dip them in flour so they are completely covered and fry in butter for 5 minutes on each side, or until golden brown. Serve with plenty of sauce messine.

Haddock fishcakes seem simple but simple food can be even more delicious than overworked complex recipes.

This is a simple satisfying winter roast. Make sure you use ready-peeled vacuum-packed chestnuts to save you the pain and boredom of doing them yourself.

100g/3½oz unsalted butter
2 oven-ready pheasants
500ml/17fl oz sweet cider
150ml/¼ pint double cream
32 peeled chestnuts
2 Golden Delicious apples, cored
2 tablespoons demerara sugar
50ml/2fl oz Calvados
salt and freshly ground black pepper

SERVES 4

Roast pheasant with glazed apples, chestnuts and Calvados sauce

Smear 50g/2oz of the butter on to the 2 birds and season with salt and pepper. Roast in a preheated oven, 200°C (400°F), Gas Mark 6, for 30–45 minutes depending on their size, or until cooked to you liking. Allow them to rest for 15 minutes somewhere warm before carving.

While the birds are roasting, pour the cider into a saucepan and boil until about 3 tablespoonfuls of concentrated cider remain. Then add the cream, boil again, season with salt and pepper and put to one side.

After the pheasants have cooked for 25 minutes, tip the chestnuts into the roasting tin with the birds and stir around; they will roast away while the bird finishes off.

Cut the apples in half across the core hole so each half has a hole in the middle. Place the apples in a grill pan and sprinkle the sugar over them. Put a few knobs of the remaining butter on each of the halves. Cook under a preheated grill for 10–15 minutes or until golden brown and slightly puffed up. It is a good idea to baste them a couple of times with the sweet buttery juices.

Before serving remove the pheasants from the roasting tin, pour off the fat leaving the chestnuts in the tin. Place the tin on the hob with the heat on and add the Calvados. With a whisk scrape away any sticky bits from the bottom of the pan and work them into the sauce. Be careful as the alcohol may ignite. Add the cider cream sauce and bring to the boil. Pour into a saucepan along with the chestnuts ready to reheat before serving.

Carve the birds, and give each plate a breast and a leg. Garnish each plate with half an apple and spoon the hot sauce over the pheasant, giving everyone plenty of chestnuts.

Apples, chestnuts and a dram of Calvados make a plain pheasant into something very special.

If you can get some well-hung, tender venison loin then this makes a really impressive dish for a dinner party. Everything except the cooking of the venison can be done in advance and reheated when required. The important thing about pommes Anna is to get a really good even, golden crust and for the potatoes to be well pressed together. To help achieve this you will need a non-stick frying pan that is about 20–22cm/8–9 inches in diameter and 3cm/1¼ inches deep and that has an ovenproof handle. You will also need a saucepan with an ovenproof handle, or a casserole dish, with a slightly smaller diameter.

6 venison loin steaks, 200g/7oz each
oil
salt and freshly ground black pepper

JUNIPER ONION COMPOTE
3 large onions
I teaspoon crushed juniper berries
200ml/7fl oz white wine vinegar
200ml/7fl oz strong jellied chicken stock (see page 76)
200ml/7fl oz double cream

POMMES ANNA
1.5kg/3lb peeled medium potatoes
250g/8oz unsalted butter, melted
I teaspoon chopped thyme
2 garlic cloves, finely chopped

SERVES 6

Loin of venison with juniper onion compote and pommes Anna

To make the onion compote, slice the onions in half through the root end then cut them into slices 2mm/³⁄₄ inch thick. Place the whole lot in a saucepan with the juniper berries and white wine vinegar, then top up with water so that the onions are nearly covered. Put on the hob and bring it to the boil. Allow this to boil away until nearly all the vinegar and water has evaporated and all that remains is the soft pale onions. Add the stock and boil again. Let the stock reduce by half then add the cream. Season with salt and pepper. The compote is now ready. Its sharp creamy and perfumed flavour is a perfect accompaniment to the venison. Put to one side while you make the pommes Anna.

To make the pommes Anna, first, melt the butter in a small saucepan. Slice the potatoes 2mm/scant ⅛ inch thick on a mandolin. Place the potatoes in a large bowl and pour 175g/6oz of the melted butter over them. Season with salt and pepper and toss the potatoes with your fingers so they are all covered with butter.

The variety of people of all ages and their conversation, make a restaurant an important part of a community.

Place the remaining butter in the frying pan and heat it up on the hob to a medium heat. Take the pan off the heat and place one disc of potato in the centre of the pan and then, working in a circle, continue to lay out the potatoes in a spiral so that each slice overlaps the last one by half. Continue with this until the bottom of the pan is covered. Place back on the heat and let this bottom layer (that will become the top layer when turned out) colour until pale golden. Then add the rest of the potatoes in layers and intersperse the layers with the chopped thyme and garlic. Do this until the pan is level full. Press the saucepan or casserole down firmly on the potatoes, using your hands to help compact the potatoes. Now place the frying pan with saucepan or casserole on top in a preheated oven, 180°C (350°F), Gas Mark 4, and cook for 40 minutes. When cooked (you can check by sticking a knife in the potatoes to see if they are soft), unmould the potatoes from the pan by placing a plate upside down on them and inverting the whole thing. This will reveal a golden brown glistening potato cake. You can keep this warm until serving, or allow to cool and then reheat before serving.

To cook the venison, season it with salt and pepper and fry in a little oil in a frying pan over a high heat for 4–5 minutes on each side, and then allow to rest somewhere warm for 10–15 minutes before serving.

To serve, reheat the compote. Thinly slice the venison to reveal rosy pink slices and serve with a spoonful or two of the hot compote and a wedge of pommes Anna.

Above: checking the reservations book; this gives the staff a clear idea of how busy they will be and how many staff they will need. Opposite: The Oyster Bar, with its inexpensive menu, is a very democratic part of the Bibendum complex.

This warming hearty dish is great for a dinner party as it can be cooked a day or two in advance and then just has to be reheated. The soft, rich, yielding meat of the belly is enhanced by a spicy chorizo centre. The long slow cooking transforms the belly and creates a fantastic jus in which to reheat it.

300g/10oz hot cooking chorizo, skinned
8 garlic cloves, finely chopped
2 tablespoons chopped sage
1.5kg/3lb piece of pork belly, boned
1 teaspoon hot Spanish paprika
groundnut oil, for cooking
3 large onions, thinly sliced
500ml/17fl oz dry sherry
10 tomatoes, coarsely chopped
salt and freshly ground black pepper
500ml/17fl oz strong jellied chicken stock (see page 76)

SERVE 6

Slow-cooked pork belly with chorizo and sherry

Break up the chorizo in a bowl with your fingers. Add the garlic and sage and mix well.

Lay the pork belly on the table, skin side down. Sprinkle the paprika all over the flesh. Then take the chorizo meat and form a rough sausage shape and place this along the top edge of the pork belly. Roll the belly up like a Swiss roll. The chorizo will be in the centre. Take some butchers' twine and tie up the belly with loops of twine. Allow a 2–3cm/³⁄4–1¼ inch gap between pieces of string. Make sure the string is nice and tight. Season the belly with salt and pepper and heat a large frying pan. Colour the outside of the belly in the pan on the hob in a little oil. When golden brown place the belly in a casserole dish with a lid. Return the frying pan to the heat and fry the onions until golden. Deglaze the pan with the sherry and tip the whole lot on the pork. Add the tomatoes to the pot. Now top up the pot with chicken stock to come three-quarters of the way up the pork. Bring to the boil and then put the lid on and cook in a preheated oven, 140°C (275°F), Gas Mark 1, for 3–4 hours. To check that it is cooked, pierce it with a skewer or roasting fork; there should be no resistance.

Remove the pork from the pan with a slotted spoon and place on a tray. Leave to cool for 30 minutes. Next, remove the strings carefully. Now you need to wrap it in clingfilm or foil to compact it. Stretch out the foil or film over a table and place the pork on it. Roll it up tightly creating several layers. You will end up with a solid cylinder about 25cm/10 inches long and 8–10cm/3¼–4 inches thick. Leave to cool then refrigerate overnight. Strain the cooking juices through a sieve and refrigerate also.

Every pot and pan has its place in a well-planned kitchen.

To serve, lightly butter an ovenproof dish. Remove the foil or film and slice the pork into 3–4cm/1 1/4–1 3/4 inch thick slices. Place these on the bottom of the buttered dish, making sure the slices do not overlap. Boil the cooking juices in a pan and allow to reduce a bit. You want enough juice remaining to come half way up the pork slices in the ovenproof dish. Once the juices are added place in a preheated oven, 180°C (350°F), Gas Mark 4, and reheat uncovered for 20–30 minutes. You must baste the slices regularly so that they remain moist. The juices will continue to reduce a little in the oven creating a lively rich jus that will glaze the pork. Serve with boiled or mashed potatoes.

There is always a hub of activity in front of the Michelin building. There is a small counter selling fish next to the Café – it holds a lobster sale every Saturday.

Forced rhubarb comes into season after Christmas and makes a welcome change to other winter fruits. Its lovely pink colour and delicate fresh taste are a great foil to the rich, creamy panna cotta.

500ml/17fl oz double cream
65g/2½oz caster sugar
65ml/2½fl oz milk
1 vanilla pod, split
2½ oranges
2¼ gelatine leaves
25ml/1fl oz Grand Marnier
750g/1½lb rhubarb, cut into 4cm/1½-inch lengths

MAKES 5–6

Orange panna cotta with rhubarb compote

Place the cream, 60g/2¼oz of the sugar, the milk, vanilla pod and grated zest from 1 orange in a saucepan and bring to the boil. Whisk to break up the vanilla seeds, remove from the heat and leave to infuse for 2 hours. Then soak the gelatine in cold water until soft. Warm the cream again but do not boil. Stir in the softened gelatine leaves and add the Grand Marnier. Stir for 2 minutes until the gelatine is dissolved and then pass the mixture through a fine sieve. Pour the mixture into ramekins or dariole moulds. Refrigerate for at least 4 hours, to set.

To make the compote, scatter the rhubarb in the bottom of a roasting tin. You do not want the pieces piled high but rather a layer of rhubarb about 4cm/1¾ inches deep. Scatter the remaining sugar evenly over the fruit. Using a zester remove the zest of the remaining orange and scatter that over. Then squeeze the juice of all 2½ oranges over the rhubarb. Toss everything together to make sure all is evenly distributed. Then cover the tray with foil and fold the edges securely underneath the rim to ensure the steam created stays in. Bake in a preheated oven, 160°C (325°F), Gas Mark 3, for 15–20 minutes. Remove from the oven and check that the rhubarb is soft with the tip of a knife. If it is still firm cook a little longer, but remember that it is a very delicate fruit and easy to overcook – then it loses its shape and breaks up. When cooked, allow to cool completely and then refrigerate until chilled.

Serve the panna cotta turned out and surrounded with a few spoonfuls of rhubarb.

Simon (below left) oversees the busy ground floor Café and Oyster Bar.

An old-fashioned baked apple dessert may seem a little out of vogue these days. The ubiquitous individual tarte Tatin (though excellent when done properly) seems to appeal more to pastry chefs. However, when I put baked apples on the menu they fly out of the door.

6 Braeburn apples

VANILLA ICE CREAM
2 vanilla pods
500ml/17fl oz milk
6 egg yolks
175g/6oz caster sugar
500ml/17fl oz double cream

FILLING
75g/3oz candied peel
75g/3oz pitted prunes, chopped
75g/3oz sultanas
1 Braeburn apple, grated
100g/3½oz shelled, roughly chopped walnuts
50g/2oz unsalted butter
100g/3½oz dark brown sugar
25ml/1fl oz Calvados

CARAMEL SAUCE
125g/4oz caster sugar
250ml/8fl oz double cream

SERVES 6

Baked apple with caramel sauce and vanilla ice cream

To make the ice cream, split the vanilla pods in half lengthwise and scrape the black seeds into the milk. Add the pods and bring to the boil. Remove from the heat, cover and leave to infuse for 30 minutes.

Place the yolks in a bowl and add the sugar. Whisk thoroughly to create a pale cream. Now pour on the hot milk and mix. Return to the pan and heat gently, stirring until slightly thickened to a what is now a custard. Do not allow to come to the boil. Remove from the heat, add the cold cream and pass through a fine sieve. Allow to cool then churn in an ice cream machine according to the manufacturer's instructions.

To make the filling, mix all the ingredients in a bowl with your hands to form a semi-cohesive mass. Put to one side.

Baked apple – one of the simplest puddings but one of the most delicious.

Core the apples, leaving them whole. Once this is done, with a small sharp knife score a circle around the equator of each apple, being careful to only just cut the skin. This little cut will allow the apples to swell without bursting during the cooking process. Stand the apples vertically in a buttered ovenproof dish and stuff as much of the filling into each one as you can manage, then stick a walnut-size ball of the filling on the top. Bake in a preheated oven, 180°C (350°F), Gas Mark 4, for 30 minutes.

While the apples are baking, make the caramel sauce: place the sugar in a heavy-bottomed saucepan over a high heat and allow it to turn to a mahogany coloured caramel. Stir it with a wooden spoon as the caramel develops to dissolve any unmelted lumps of sugar. The darker you take the caramel the more bitter it will taste; if you like a sweeter caramel take it off the heat sooner. When the caramel has reached the desired colour remove it from the heat and add the cream carefully because it will spit and splutter. This will stop the caramel cooking any more. Now return the pan to a medium heat and stir to dissolve the lumps of caramel that will have formed. Pass this through a fine sieve and keep warm.

To serve, allow one apple per person with a generous scoop of vanilla ice cream and lots of caramel sauce.

It is the sticky caramel sauce which makes the baked apples a real treat.

Back in the mid 1980s whilst I was working in Geneva as a young chef, my parents came to visit. My father announced one day that he was going to take my mother and me to the best restaurant in the world 'or so they say!'. On my next day off, we travelled to the small village of Crissier just outside Lausanne where the celebrated chef, Fredy Girardet ran his eponymous restaurant. It was a truly memorable meal and certainly at that young age was the best restaurant I had ever been to. For dessert, as well as a trolley full of different ice creams, we had this simple but outstanding tart that has become a firm favourite of mine ever since.

750g/1 ½ lb ready made all-butter puff pastry
1 egg, lightly beaten
400g/13oz caster sugar
100g/3½ oz plain flour
1 litre/1 ¾ pints Jersey cream
1 tablespoon ground cinnamon
50g/2oz unsalted butter

SERVES 8

Tarte vaudoise à la crème

Grease a 26cm/10½-inch tart case with a removable base and sides no higher than 2.5cm/1 inch.

Roll out the pastry as thinly as you can (2–3mm/about ⅛ inch is ideal) and line the tart case. Trim the edges neatly and prick the base all over with a fork. Take care to make lots and lots of holes so that when cooked the pastry does not puff up but stays thin and crispy with plenty of layers.

Now line the case with a sheet of greaseproof paper and fill with baking beans. Cook in a preheated oven, 200°C (400°F), Gas Mark 6, for 25 minutes or until golden and crisp all over. Remove the paper and beans. Paint the inside of the tart case with the egg, using a pastry brush. The egg will fill and seal any holes from the pricking. Return the tart case to the oven for 3 minutes to cook the egg. Remove the tart case from the oven, and increase the oven temperature to 220°C (425°F), Gas Mark 7.

Next mix the sugar, flour and cream together and whilst stirring, bring to the boil, reduce the heat and allow this to boil gently and cook the flour. After 5–10 minutes the cream will thicken to the consistency of custard. Remove it from the heat and pour the mixture into the tart case. It will not fill the case but will cover the bottom in a layer about 1cm/½ inch thick. Now tip the ground cinnamon into a fine sieve and bang the sieve against the edge of your hand over the tart to shower the tart top with a layer of cinnamon. Drop the knobs of butter evenly over the tart.

Bake for 20 minutes or until golden. Allow to cool completely before serving.

Top right: Michael Hamlyn, a director and shareholder. Terence started the restaurant with his father, Paul, and Simon Hopkinson 21 years ago. It is good to have his youth, keen interests and involvement.

Although this is a somewhat time consuming cake to make, once mastered it is not as daunting as it may seem. This is a rich smooth cake and even though this recipe makes enough to serve twelve lots of people will want seconds. At the restaurant we make this recipe in a 20cm square 3.5cm/1½-inch deep mousse frame. Alternatively you could line a similarly-sized springform cake ring with greaseproof paper and use that.

SPONGE
50g/2oz caster sugar
2 eggs
50g/2oz plain flour
Amaretto liqueur (see method)

WHITE MOUSSE
375ml/13fl oz double cream
200g/7oz white chocolate, chopped
3 egg yolks

DARK MOUSSE
520ml/17½ fl oz double cream
200g/7oz extra-bitter dark chocolate, chopped
40g/1½ oz caster sugar
4 egg yolks

AMARETTO CREME ANGLAISE *(optional)*
6 egg yolks
100g/3½ oz caster sugar
1 vanilla pod
500ml/17fl oz milk
50ml/2fl oz Amaretto liqueur

SERVES 12

Marbled chocolate mousse cake with Amaretto crème Anglaise

The sponge forms the base for your mousse to sit on. To make it, whisk the sugar and eggs together on full speed in your kitchen mixer until a large firm mousse is formed. Now sift the flour onto the egg mixture and fold in with a spatula, trying to keep as much air in the sponge as possible. Take a baking sheet large enough to hold the mousse ring and line the sheet with greaseproof paper. Using a palette knife spread the sponge out, covering the paper with a 4mm/scant ¼-inch thick layer. Bake in a preheated oven, 185°C (350°F), Gas Mark 4, for 10 minutes or until set. Allow to cool on a rack, without removing the lining paper.

Although the food is usually quite simple at Bibendum, this fancy marbled cake is an exception.

Then place the sponge back on the baking sheet with the greaseproof paper uppermost. Carefully peel away the paper and place the mousse ring over the sponge. With a knife trim away the bits that stick out. Put a splash of Amaretto in a glass and, with a pastry brush, paint the sponge to moisten it. Put to one side.

Both mousses are made in exactly the same way. It is best to make the white mousse first as it will have to sit in a jug whilst you make the dark mousse and it will take longer to set. You will end up with two thick, but still just pourable mousses in separate jugs. Anyway, back to making them. To make the white mousse, heat half of the double cream and all the white chocolate in a double boiler, or a bowl placed over a saucepan of gently simmering water. When the chocolate has melted, remove from the heat and stir in the egg yolks. Allow to cool to room temperature and then add the remaining double cream and whip in a food mixer on medium speed, or using a hand whisk, to soft ribbon stage – when you lift the whisk out of the mixture the mousse should leave ribbon marks on the surface when the whisk is waved over it. Transfer this mixture into a jug and quickly make the dark mousse.

To make the dark mousse, follow the method for the white mousse, adding the sugar when you put the chocolate and the first half of the cream in the double boiler.

Now, assemble the cake. Taking a jug in each hand, pour the mousses onto the cake base in swirls, to make a marble effect. Refrigerate for at least 6 hours.

To make the crème Anglaise, in a mixing bowl, whisk the egg yolks and sugar together to form a pale cream. Split the vanilla pod lengthwise and scrape out the black seeds into a saucepan. Add the pod and milk and bring to the boil. Pour over the egg and whisk until just mixed. Return the mixture to a low heat and stir with the whisk until it starts to thicken. Allow it to get close to boiling without allowing it to boil, then remove from the heat and pass through a fine sieve. Now stir in the Amaretto and allow to cool to room temperature before chilling

To serve, carefully remove the mousse ring or sides of the springform cake tin and serve the cake in slices, accompanied by the Amaretto crème Anglaise, if liked.

The marbled chocolate topping on this cake is a real work of art.

Acknowledgements

We are grateful to all the staff and suppliers who currently work and have worked with Bibendum over the last 21 years and who have helped to make it such a remarkable Restaurant, Oyster Bar and Café.

We are particularly proud of the many past members of staff who have gone on to open and run successful restaurants around the UK and the world. Bibendum has been and continues to be a great place for developing talent.

None of this would have been possible if Michelin had not built this beautiful building in 1909 and if the extraordinary heritage of innovation, humour and foresight that they have demonstrated over the last hundred years had not been available to inspire us.

We are very conscious that we are the keepers of the Michelin brand in this important corner of London and we continue to respect it. We feel as if Monsieur Bibendum is our Father. Thanks for the key to the door, Dad.

TERENCE CONRAN, SIMON HOPKINSON & MICHAEL HAMLYN

A front view of the Michelin Building at night in all its glory.

Soupe de Poissons with rouille and croûtons. 10.50

Escargots de Bourgogne. 19.50

Salad of thinly sliced pink veal with leeks vinaigrette,
pousse, poached egg and tarragon sabayon. 12.00

Grilled scallops with wild garlic greens, lemon and
thyme risotto. 15.00

Bibendum terrine. 10.50

Poached oysters in champagne and chive velouté
with spring vegetables. 17.50

Deep fried chicken livers with sauce gribiche. 11.00

Terrine of foie gras with Armagnac jelly. 19.50

Crab and artichoke salad with saffron vinaigrette. 15.00

Gravadlax and roll mop herrings with horseradish
mousse, pickled cucumber and beetroot. 12.00

Steak tartare. 14.50

Open ravioli of lambs sweetbreads with shallot purée,
spinach and sauce poivrade. 12.50

Endive salad with walnuts, croûtons and Roquefort
dressing 10.50

Warm salad of smoked eel with Jersey royals, crisp
pancetta and soft boiled quails egg. 14.50

Prices include V.A.T. An optional service charge of 12½%
will be added to your bill.

Chef: Matthew Harris